AN
INTRODUCTION
TO
HOMILETICS

AN INTRODUCTION TO HOMILETICS

DONALD
E.
DEMARAY

BAKER BOOK HOUSE
GRAND RAPIDS, MICHIGAN

PHOTOLITHOPRINTED BY CUSHING - MALLOY, INC.
ANN ARBOR, MICHIGAN, UNITED STATES OF AMERICA

To
C. Rowan Lunsford
my first teacher of homiletics

ACKNOWLEDGMENTS

Warm appreciation is expressed to the University Library, Cambridge, England, for use of its resources. Tyndale House, Cambridge, provided through its excellent facilities, residential and literary, a haven where the first draft of this book was typed in the summer of 1972.

Further thanks go to the Officers of Administration, Asbury Theological Seminary, for sabbatical time to devote to this project. Especially I wish to express gratitude to the Seminary students for full and lively dialog, out of which inevitably comes a fresh look at the laws of pulpit work.

To D. Elton Trueblood must go very many thanks for encouraging me—in more ways than one—in the pursuit of written communication. He is a never-failing source of inspiration.

PREFACE

Dividing itself naturally into three parts, this work treats the preacher (his preparation), the sermon (the actual sermon construction), and the preaching (the delivery of the sermon). In this way we are introduced step by step into the field of homiletics. With the reading of this volume, it is hoped earnestly that the young theologian in college or seminary will begin and continue the development of his skills as a public preacher, that the lay preacher struggling to find help will be materially assisted, and that the man who has been in the ministry for some time will discover new techniques and renewed inspiration.

The posture of the book is evangelical—that without apology. The role of the sovereign God is indicated at the very outset in the discussion on the call to preach. The central place of Scripture is assumed throughout, as is personal religious experience.

An attempt is also made to bring together the old and the new. Classical homiletics and rhetoric still claim their ancient hold on God's men, and a changing world, with new communication perspectives, demands our careful attention. In other words, Jowett and Brooks help us, but so do Halverson and Rees. Put somewhat differently, the classical rhetoricians may yet speak to us helpfully, but so do the modern communication specialists.

Preaching is God's method of turning men to God. The fervent prayer of the author is that preachers young and old will find in this volume skills divine and human for making the gospel winsome, and thereby capture many fish in their nets.

DONALD E. DEMARAY
On the eve of Reformation Day

CONTENTS

PART ONE:

THE PREACHER

I. THE PREPARATION OF THE PREACHER

God "never gives His servants a work to do without also giving them all needed help," said F. B. Meyer. Truer words were never spoken. God gives and God helps. The essential task of preparation to preach is fundamentally a divine undertaking. Cooperate we must. Initiate and guide we cannot; that is God's twin function.

GOD CALLS THE PREACHER

Not man, but God. That is the imperative place of beginning in any discussion of the call to preach.

(1) THE CALL IS INITIATED BY GOD. To preach is God's choice before it is mine. Notice how Paul begins the longest of his epistles: "Paul, a servant of Jesus Christ, called . . . set apart . . ." (Rom. 1:1). He is called "to be an apostle," he says, and set apart "for the gospel of God."

When God initiates the call, a sense of inner urgency results. John Henry Jowett, in the classic, *The Preacher: His Life and Work,* puts it perfectly when he says that an authentic call is "not a preference among alternatives. Ultimately he has no alternative: all other possibilities become dumb: there is only one clear call sounding forth as the imperative summons of the eternal God."

A fascinating drama took place at a meeting of college and university presidents. President Charles Odegard of the University of Washington was presiding. He had instructed his secretary not to bother him under any circumstances. But to his amazement she broke into the meeting and asked him to come to the phone. Sternly he spoke, "I told you not to. . . ." "But," she said haltingly, "it's the president of the United States."

13

Ah! That was different. He lost no time getting to the phone. The President himself had called.

That sense of being "under orders," as L. P. Jacks phrased it, is exactly what Paul felt when he cried, "Necessity is laid upon me. Woe is me if I preach not the gospel!" (I Corinthians 9:16b). Methodist Bishop Simpson rightly said of the commissioned man that "God requires him to do this work at the peril of his own soul." That, said the bishop, is the nature of the call in its strongest form.

(2) WHEN "THE CALL" HAS NOT BEEN INITIATED BY GOD. Samuel Moffett, famed missionary to Korea, pled with his five sons, "Don't go into the ministry if you can help it!" All became preachers, but at God's beckoning. Many a son has been "called" by a father only to find the decision wrong. It appears some are called by a doting aunt, or a supposedly wise pastor who detects public gifts in a man. This is all to no avail. Far wiser the mother who explained why her boy, graduate of a Scottish theological college, did not take a pastorate his first year out of training: "He's no' felt the call yet." But the following year he did and went out to preach with the blessing of God Himself.

The specter of double-mindedness is ever over the man not authentically called of God. The sure mark of the truly summoned man is unequivocal surrender to the Caller. The proof of both call and surrender is an anchored preacher, anchored and immovable in the very storms of his life. The plain fact of the matter is this: a man simply cannot "hang in there" with any kind of consistency, without the firmly rooted conviction that he is in very fact working for the Sovereign God.

Any man in the ministry very long knows full well that the temptations to go under in the storms are many. Here is a college boy who was called, he said, but who never quite gave himself to the task of preparation; today he is hopelessly entwined in business and domestic affairs and will never preach. Here is another who, in fact, does preach; he maintains a little mission church but has never given himself wholly to God or the mission. His annual conference reports are monotonously the same: "The membership is about what it was last year." Here is one more, a man who preached for a time but who finally developed a career in sales.

Either God did not call these men to the ministry or they did not respond with an eternal Yes. Whichever the case, morale collapsed, the anchor gave way, and each succeeded in escaping the hard business of fighting sin in the name of God.

We must go deeper still, and become even more specific. Take the actual temptations that threaten the minister. Here, in the first place, is the constant and nagging desire for *privacy*. "If only I could have a bit of peace and quiet," says many a man within the precincts of his own house. The phone rings, the doorbell sounds, the committee meetings abound—fatigue sets in quickly. There simply must be resources with which to cope with all this busyness. Yes, there are. Not the least of the resources is the call. The call sustains motivation and in the most trying of circumstances opens the door of the heart to the still small voice, "You did not choose me, but I chose you and appointed you that you should go and bear fruit. . . ." That, as nothing else, will hold a man steady when the storms of busyness threaten the very citadel of his soul.

Take, in the second place, the temptation to make *money*. And who is not confronted squarely with that temptation? Anyone with fairly good management capacity—and capable ministers often have that—can find executive positions that pay better than the ministry. How inviting other offers look! But the called man has an anchor to hold him fast.

A third temptation induces the minister to worry about what will happen to his *family*. Will living in a fishbowl damage my children? Will my wife be able to tolerate the demands of the minister's house? Will there be enough money to finance my children's education? A thousand questions come, but the man whose call is of God has an anchor to hold him immovable. He puts his trust in God to care for the family, and his faith is strengthened by the many minis-

ters' families which have indeed been cared for in the most
beautiful way.

There is a fourth temptation, persistent and insidious. It is
the ever-present temptation of *over-identification*. While it
may and does present itself elsewhere and at different times,
it presents itself very vividly in the counseling room. No
moral indiscretion may ever flower, though many a minister,
sad to say, has found himself caught in a difficult situation.
Lack of identification results in inability to render the desired
and needed aid. Over-identification drains one emotionally
and seriously diverts thought and energy. Sigmund Freud
found himself followed from one town to another by over-
dependent women who could not stand on their own two feet.
The wise minister keeps himself at "professional distance,"
but leaves no doubt as to his sincere desire to give spiritual
advice. In this way he does both himself and his people a
great favor. That wise communication pattern is the fruit of
the conviction of a divine calling.

The temptations which intrude themselves in a thousand
ways and forms are too numerous to treat with any kind of
completeness. There is the loss of faith in people: they *do* let
you down. Then there is the temptation to discouragement:
the devil knows that a disillusioned man cannot serve God
wholeheartedly and fruitfully. The subtle drawing power of
prestige is ever present, and the devastating effect of pride
is demonstrated over and over. Add to these the whole complex of involvements in the ministry. It is quite enough to
overwhelm any minister! And they will indeed overwhelm
him unless he has the sure conviction that God has called
him to preach and to serve.

(3) THE CALL IS TO BE AN AMBASSADOR. An ambassador
is, in the correct sense, a proud man: and he should be. He
is proud of his country, and proud to represent *his* country
in the country to which he has been called. The ambassador's
manner immediately reflects that normal and healthy pride.

After all, a minister represents the King. Everyone knew
that Bishop Robert Warren occupied himself with the King's

business. His personal grooming and platform presence announced, with never a hint of the overbearing: "I am God's man and take thorough delight in my position." One wonders seriously if the milquetoast ministers, who seem to abound, have any concept whatsoever of the ambassadorship of the called. The apologetic, weak-kneed, embarrassed, and timid preacher whose language is freely punctuated with "maybe" and "I think" and "perhaps" had better discover the Source of Authority, or get out of the ministry. Says Phillips Brooks in his usual manly style: "The timid minister is as bad as the timid surgeon. If you are afraid of men and a slave to their opinion, go and do something else. Go and make shoes to fit them. Go even and paint pictures which are bad, but which suit their bad taste. But do not keep on all your life preaching sermons which shall say not what God sent you to declare, but what they hire you to say."

Such a shy "ambassador" is no ambassador at all. But the man "conscripted" by God Himself goes about his task with boldness and with a noble bearing. The call of the King and his unhesitating belief in the King's backing give him a sense of royal confidence. He is a called ambassador.

GOD ANOINTS THE PREACHER

As Saul was anointed king, so God's preachers are anointed ambassadors. What is the meaning of that anointing?

(1) THE CLUE TO ANOINTING—JESUS. Jesus, the very son of God, engaged in ministry only after the special touch of the Spirit. Indeed, the very term *Messiah* means "anointed one." The anointing came at His baptism; the record in Luke 3:21-22 reads: "Now when all the people were baptized, and when Jesus also had been baptized and was praying, the heaven was opened, and the Holy Spirit descended upon him in bodily form, as a dove, and a voice came from heaven, 'Thou art my beloved Son; with thee I am well pleased.' " Significantly, we have the following words immediately after the account of His baptism and anointing in the Spirit:

"Jesus, when he began his ministry . . ." (v. 23). *Began* is the important word; He began his ministry only after His anointing. His anointing explains the announcement to the synagogue congregation at Nazareth: "The Spirit of the Lord is upon me . . ." (4:18a). This is also why, significantly enough, He could come through the Temptation (4:1-13) and return "in the power of the Spirit into Galilee" (4:14a).

There is no ministry, much less the successful one coping with its peculiar temptations, without the preparation that comes with God's Spirit. The anointing is symbolized in the laying-on-of-hands in ordination, but the actual divine anointing, or its flower, may not come at the time of public ordination. The fuller meaning came to W. E. Sangster some years after his entrance into the ministry. His son Paul, in *Dr. Sangster* (pp. 89-92, 109-10), describes what he says was his father's most crucial religious experience. Vividly he tells of his father's retiring to the attic for earnest prayer over a considerable period of time. He struggled. Reputation and an academic degree threatened to usurp God's place. Ruthlessly honest with himself, he admitted, "I wanted degrees more than knowledge, and praise rather than equipment for service" (p. 90). At last came the victory and the full surrender. Sangster experienced a baptism of the Spirit which was to change the course of his ministry, a course well known to students of his life. It is significant that Sangster's anointing for service came in prayer, even as Jesus' experience (Luke 3:21). Paul Sangster puts it in plain language: "The secret" to his surrender Dr. Sangster found "in prayer" (p. 91).

Just there, in that word *surrender,* lies the key. During the temptation of Jesus the devil put his finger on the spots most likely to be vulnerable: (1) authority: Jesus could command nations; (2) power: Jesus could turn stones to bread; (3) popularity: sensationally He could throw Himself from great heights. Authority, power, popularity had to yield to the Cross. That meant nothing more nor less than the full surrender of Himself to the task for which He had entered the world.

E. Stanley Jones records the issue in language vivid to the called man or woman. Says he: "We have seen many a missionary leave loved ones, friends, home, business, prospects, and come to other lands and find that he had given up everything except—just himself. Self was still there, assertive and jealous of its place and honor. Jesus asks us to lay down that last thing. For this life of complete liberty cannot be lived apart from the acceptance of a complete law—the law of self-abandonment. Only then are we able to say: 'I do not want anything, therefore I am afraid of nothing.' Only as we lose ourselves do we find ourselves again. We become utterly poor and yet possess all things. We take the cross and find an Easter morning. Self-surrender is the door to abundant life and there is no other door" (*The Christ of the Round Table,* p. 327).

The very thing which we by nature do not want to do— and indeed cannot do in our own strength—is to lose our lives. But with God's help we do make that complete surrender, miracle that it literally is! Then God comes with anointing power, brings our best self to flower, and supplies fulfillment in His service.

No one has couched this truth in more eloquent language than the German theologian, Dietrich Bonhoeffer, who, in his book, *The Cost of Discipleship,* speaks with prophetic insight into his own destiny: "When Christ calls a man, he bids him come and die . . . in fact every command of Jesus is a call to die, with all our affections and lusts. But we do not want to die, and therefore Jesus Christ and his call are necessarily our death as well as our life."

Just here is the secret of power in preaching. Without anointing and surrender, the preacher's words are devoid of penetration and thrust. With anointing his words become the Word of God, ". . . living and active, sharper than any two-edged sword, piercing to the division of soul and spirit, of joints and marrow, and discerning the thoughts and intentions of the heart" (Heb. 4:12).

(2) THE MARK OF THE ANOINTED MAN—AUTHORITY.

After Jesus had read and commented on the Isaiah passage in the Nazareth synagogue, He went down to Capernaum and there the people were ". . . astonished at his teaching, for his word was with power" (Luke 4:32). "And they were all amazed," the text reads a bit further down (v. 36), "and said one to another, 'What is this word? For with authority and power he commands the unclean spirits, and they come out.' " That, after He had cast a demon out of a man in the synagogue (v. 33-36).

Our Lord's inaugural address in the Nazareth synagogue makes clear His mission and precisely what His authority and anointing were designed to do. Power is intended for divine purposes. What are they?

Quoting from Isaiah and speaking of Himself, Jesus says, "The Spirit of the Lord is upon me, because he has anointed me to preach good news to the poor." That is *number one: to preach good news to the poor*. Notice the key terms: "Preach . . . good news . . . poor."

To "preach" means to announce . . . as the town crier used to broadcast the news . . . as today's radio and television newscasters deliver news. John Baillie the Scot used to say that news cannot dawn on one; it must be announced. If I wish to know the 7 o'clock news in the morning, I must turn on the radio and listen to the announcer as he reads the news. I cannot get it unless it is told me.

Unlike most of today's media news, the *gospel* is *good news*. Unlike most of today's preaching which is mere good advice, the gospel is glad tidings (Old English *godspell*-glad tidings). The glad tidings is the news that Jesus came into the world and suffered, died, and arose that we might be saved. The Cross, yes—that is the evil Jesus had to endure and overcome; but also the resurrection—that is the demonstration of God's victory over evil. That fundamental truth, that God is victorious over evil, is the good news which people want and need to hear.

The final key term is *poor*. Some words in Scripture have double meaning; here *poor* refers to both poverty of spirit and means. The two often go together. Probably for most who heard the first beatitude, the twin poverties were reality. "Blessed are the poor in spirit," said Jesus, "for theirs is the kingdom of heaven" (Matt. 5:3). The Kingdom of Heaven would come to both heart and hand, as He made clear later in the Sermon on the Mount, and as Christian history with its developed worship centers and welfare agencies demonstrates. There is the authoritative gospel of overcoming evil with good.

This preaching of good news to the poor was Jesus' task while on earth. It is the weighty responsibility and blessed privilege of the called and anointed preacher today.

Number two: "He sent me to proclaim release to the captives" (Luke 4:18c). Release is the hoped-for product of gospel preaching. People are by nature imprisoned by sin and its effects. They are hemmed in by themselves, by a warped image of God, by what their neighbors think of them. Only the gospel possesses power sufficient to break down prison walls and set people free. Listen to this bit of gospel preaching which exemplifies the point at hand: "Surrender to Christ saves you, on the one hand, from egotistic self-assertion, always wanting to occupy the center of attention, and on the other hand, from shyness which is always shrinking and thinking, 'What do they think of me?' It saves you from self-consciousness and from herd-consciousness because you have Christ-consciousness. You are not a worm nor a wonder. You are the ordinary becoming the extraordinary, all due to Him. So you can be yourself because you are His self. You are free to be" (E. Stanley Jones, *Victory through Surrender,* p. 46).

People respond to that kind of preaching, spoken with divine authority by the anointed preacher. They make their surrender to the Christ, and breathe the free air of Christian freedom. Jesus came to proclaim release to captives. That is no less the task of every preacher called of God.

Number Three: "And recovering of sight to the blind." Apparently Jesus intended this to be taken both spiritually and physically. In His own ministry He preached the recovery of spiritual sight—"Ye must be born again" (John 3)—and He healed the blind (John 9). Take the latter first. If we can use healing from blindness as symbolic of the whole mending ministry, then we see here the implication for one dimension of gospel proclamation. Jesus plainly taught us to teach, preach, and heal (Luke 9:2; Matt. 28:20); and an examination of His own ministry proves He did all three. True preaching is therapeutic. D. Martyn Lloyd-Jones tells of the paralytic girl whose malady was the product of hysteria. Subsequent to coming under the influence of gospel preaching, she recovered her ability to walk and continues in good health (*Preaching and Preachers,* pp. 37-38). There are times to be more specific, actually preaching on Christian healing, and for us to do as James instructs us to do (James 5:13 ff.). Jesus came to give "sight to the blind."

But basic to all is the recovery of sight to the spiritually blind. John Wesley likened the coming of spiritual sight to the emergence of physical sight in a newborn child. While still in the fetal stage, sight is impossible; with birth comes sight. There is a sense in which the preacher of the gospel is a doctor: he delivers the newborn babe in Christ. The work of an obstetrician can be an exciting business! To watch a newborn babe actually see that to which he once was blind is indeed exciting. So can the work of the preacher be exciting as he witnesses the opening of the eyes of the spiritually blind.

George Whitefield was attacked verbally with this question: "Why do you preach so frequently on the text, 'Ye must be born again'?" Whitefield, who had preached on the text literally dozens of times, replied forthrightly, "Because, sir, ye must be born again." Let that divine imperative grip a man, and he will preach to see the blind come into the Kingdom with full vision.

Number Four: "To set at liberty those who are oppressed" (Luke 4:18e). The older translation refers to the "broken victims" being set "free." Jesus here refers to the broken in spirit, the crushed. It is interesting indeed that in the ministry of our Lord, the brokenness of a man, not his status, caught His attention. Here was a leper; Jesus touched him even though Jewish law forbad touching a leper, and even commanded Jews to keep at some distance from the diseased. Here is a woman caught in the clutches of adultery (John 4); her status—race, sex, sin—could not deter Him from helping a hurting woman. Here is a rich young ruler struggling to find life; though wealthy, he was oppressed and, therefore, not at liberty. Jesus pointed the way to freedom. That is what He came to do. That is what today's preacher is called to do.

Number Five: "To proclaim the acceptable year of the Lord." The New English Bible reads, "To proclaim the year of the Lord's favour." "Year" means "the age of fulfilment or Messianic era" (G. W. H. Lampe on Luke in *Peake's Commentary on the Bible*. General Editor and N. T. Editor, Matthew Black; O. T. Editor, H. H. Rowley. London: Thomas Nelson and Sons Ltd., 1962, p. 828). Jesus had come at the propitious time in history—just the right time, God's time. He Himself introduced the gospel era; now that He has come, any time is the right time to tell people the good news about what God has done in Jesus. Paul says with intense feeling and deep conviction: "Working together with him, then, we entreat you not to accept the grace of God in vain. For he says, 'At the acceptable time I have listened to you, and helped you on the day of salvation.' Behold, now is the acceptable time; behold, now is the day of salvation" (II Cor. 6:1-2).

There are, of course, "seasons of the Spirit," times God breaks through in unusual and special ways. The mighty days of the Wesleyan Revival, the transforming periods called the Welch Revivals, the explosions of spiritual power in the days of Finney, and in our own time the first-centurylike atmosphere of miracle—these all represent seasons of the Spirit. The prepared man will take advantage of such times, and speak with a freshly fired heart, striking while the iron is hot. But he will also preach faithfully "out of season," speaking truths both "old and new" from his treasury, thus saving the lost and nurturing the saved.

Jesus employed His Spirit-given authority (1) to preach good news to the poor, (2) to proclaim release to the captives, (3) to give sight to the blind, (4) to set at liberty those who are oppressed, and (5) to proclaim the acceptable year of the Lord. Jesus passed on His authority to Peter and His church: "I will give you the keys of the kingdom of heaven, and whatever you bind on earth shall be bound in heaven, and whatever you loose on earth shall be loosed in heaven" (Matt. 16:19). When the anointed preacher declares the mighty acts of God to the poor, unreleased, blind, and oppressed people in this gospel era, God's Spirit opens hearts to riches in Christ Jesus, to freedom, to sight, and to liberty from oppression. Forgiveness and healing come through the lips of the minister as he preaches the eternal Word. The man of God has special authority for such New Testament ministry. "Take thou authority . . . ," says the bishop at the service of ordination. Authority is given to preach the Word of God and administer the sacraments; in a word, to preach, teach, and heal.

Quaker founder George Fox, anointed and prophetic, illustrates such authority and instructs us in the management of of it with due humility. William Penn, in his famous preface to the first edition of Fox's *Journal,* declares: "And truly, I must say, that though God had visibly clothed him with a divine preference and authority, and indeed his very presence expressed a religious majesty; yet he never abused it, but held his place in the Church of God with great meekness and most engaging humility and moderation. For upon all occasions, like his blessed Master, he was a servant to all . . . his authority was inward and not outward, and . . . he got it and kept it by the love of God and the power of an endless life." (Preface to George Fox's *Journal,* London: Thomas Northcott, 1694.)

GOD ILLUMINES THE PREACHER

With the Holy Spirit in anointing power comes not only the gift of authority but the grace of illumination. That enlightenment of the mind and spirit comes specially tailored for each individual, and at God's time, pace, and place. Sometimes He operates like the erupting insight which psychologists call Gestalt: the pieces of a puzzle come together and at last the picture reveals itself. Other times the picture parts fall together only gradually. However it takes place, the grand truths of life and the gospel form themselves in the mind of the one called of God with a completeness sufficient for a working theology. But, excitingly enough, he never knows when some additional bit of illumination will come to enlarge and enrich a picture he thought finished at an earlier point in his pilgrimage. The capacity for growth in illumination results from the continuing life in the Spirit.

Here we discuss a pair of pictures, illumined for us by the Spirit in Scripture and experience. The two provide absolutely essential perspectives for the one who would undertake the preaching task, and illustrate the fact of illumination.

PICTURE NUMBER 1: A HIGH VIEW OF PREACHING. Paul shares his own moment of Gestalt about preaching: "For since, in the wisdom of God, the world did not know God through wisdom, it pleased God through the folly of what we preach to save those who believe" (I Cor. 1:21). It is crystal clear that Paul believed greatly in preaching. One of the marks of the Pauline preacher, in the first century or in our own, is his unwavering faith in the preached Word.

It must be so. Can you imagine, even vaguely, one who is not quite sure of the preached Word lifting up his voice and speaking with robust earnestness the truth about the living God? Could it be that the weak and superficial theology so prevalent in much of the twentieth century causes our anemic proclamations? Is it just possible that the weak-kneed, spineless situation ethics of our time, embraced by many a minister, is to blame for tiny voices and pretty essays from the pulpit? Could it be that not a few gathered Christian communities no longer excite the preacher to proclaim the Word with power because he himself has lost his enthusiasm?

But let a young preacher discover, not from a book but experientially, what happens when the Word of God is truly preached, and he will be excited. Let him see twisted, turned, and tragic lives lifted to a whole new level of existence, and he will believe in preaching. Let him observe first hand a broken family healed under the preaching of the healing Word, and he will believe in preaching. Let him witness, in the very crucible of life, an innocent child of God discovering the reality of sin and the awfulness of evil, and on top of that hard truth, learning that God has in fact done something about the whole miserable business; the young minister who sees that for himself will believe in preaching.

Any preacher who witnesses the power of the announced Good News will be hard put to preach a dull sermon. He sees for himself that preaching is God's ordained means of winning men to himself and nurturing them in the faith. Sangster puts it exactly right when he observes that preaching is God's "supreme method in making his message known." If the devil can get us to doubt that basic dictum of the faith, he is certain to see his cause succeed. But he will have an enormously difficult time getting anywhere if the minister proceeds with the conviction that preaching is the very Incarnate Word of God coming through human lips. If he comes to the dynamic realization that preaching is truth, actual truth, flowing through his own personality, weak and frail though it may be, he will preach with prophetic fire.

Let him believe *that,* and the foundation of a sound theology of preaching is his.

PICTURE NUMBER 2: A CLEAR VIEW OF NEW TESTAMENT PREACHING. It is absolutely essential to grasp the real content of pulpit declaration, for only then will one know what to say from the pulpit.

The substance of New Testament preaching is found by isolating the common denominators of the earliest sermons of the church, preserved in the Acts of the Apostles. The common denominators are defined by two Greek terms, *kerygma* and *didache.*

Kerygma, related to the infinitive *keryssein,* is heralded proclamation; the New Testament herald is the *kerux.* The function of the *kerux* is, in Alan Richardson's language, "The telling of news to people who had not heard before . . ." (*A Theological Word Book of the Bible,* p. 171). James S. Stewart helps clarify the meaning of the term *kerygma* when he says that, "preaching exists not for the propagating of views, opinions and ideals, but for the proclamation of the mighty acts of God" (*Heralds of God,* p. 5).

For further clarification of the nature of New Testament preaching it is necessary to segregate the teachings preached in the early church, a task several scholars have undertaken in this century, C. H. Dodd of Cambridge making a pioneer attempt. In our own time, Robert Mounce has lifted out the doctrinal items in a helpful way. If his analysis of *kerygma* were to be charted, the picture would look like this:

KERYGMA IS
    A proclamation of the
        1. Death,
        2. Resurrection, and
        3. Exaltation of our Lord,
        4. All seen as the fulfillment of prophecy, and
        5. Involving man's responsibility;
    The resultant evaluation of Jesus as both
        6. Lord, and
        7. Christ; and
        8. Repent, and
        9. Receive forgiveness of sins.

Dr. Mounce provides this analysis for us in his excellent volume, *The Essential Nature of New Testament Preaching.* John R. W. Stott, in his lectures, *The Preacher's Portrait,* follows Mounce and supplies his own commentary on the *kerygma.*

To stop with *kerygma* is to paint only a partial picture of

New Testament preaching. Dr. Mounce proceeds to clarify
the second of the common denominators, the term *didache,*
which refers to the teaching phase of the preacher's task.

Earlier, following C. H. Dodd's *The Apostolic Preaching,*
kerygma and *didache* were segregated quite completely—the
one being preaching to the unconverted, the other to the converted. More recently authorities such as Brilioth, Stott, and
especially Mounce, have been convinced that strict separation
is both artificial and impossible. This accounts for the term
didactic-kerygma.

Mounce gives the following helpful definition of *didache:*
"Teaching is the expounding in detail of that which is proclaimed." Wrapped in this definition is his rationale for the
conviction that *kerygma* is foundation and *didache* superstructure. It remains true that *didache* is instruction to converts; but it is more. It is equally true that *kerygma* is proclamation to non-Christians; but telling the mighty acts of
God builds up the converted too. *Kerygma* and *didache* be-
long together.

Made graphic in charted form, the picture would emerge
this way:

DIDACHE AND KERYGMA

Kerygma: Public proclamation to non-Christians.
Didache: Instruction to converts.

Didactic-Kerygma: The expounding in detail of that
which is proclaimed.

Kerygma is foundation.
Didache is superstructure.

Kerygma explained and applied is *Didache* and ever
necessary.
Didache collapses without the *Kerygmatic* footings.

The task of the preacher is, therefore, twofold: to win
converts and to nurture those converts. To win converts the
preacher is obliged to proclaim the eternal truths of God's

Word, involving sin and judgment in God's presence, spelling out God's salvation through Christ and His cross, calling for decision to accept what God has done in Christ and to live accordingly.

To nurture converts one must preach the substance of the Christian faith, explaining how Christians are to live in the world with God, themselves, and their fellow man.

Preaching that attends to both—*didactic-kerygmatic* preaching—brings wholeness, healing. Preaching overweighted on the *kerygmatic* side, emphasizing conversion to the exclusion of nurture, produces ethically sick Christians. Preaching overweighted on the *didactic* side, focusing on the social implications of the gospel, results in theoretically sick Christians. The New Testament preacher keeps the two in balance.

II. THE DISCIPLINES OF THE PREACHER

Scottish theologian John Baillie had, in his study room at home, all the symbols of personal discipline. (1) There were the books he read, thousands of them. (2) There was the desk at which he wrote books, articles, letters. (3) There was a kneeling altar with prayerbook desk, where he celebrated daily the life of devotion. (4) Yes, and there was even an easy chair with accompanying foot-rest—a little segment of his library room for relaxation. (5) Finally, there was the telephone, symbol of the listening ear.

You will notice the flavor of careful stewardship of time. Baillie never allowed himself the luxury of frittering away the moments (nor did he, on the other hand, permit a neurotic conscientiousness about time).

THE PREACHER'S LIBRARY

John Baillie was a great reader. If any one translated Bacon's proverb into practice, it was Baillie. Said Bacon, "Reading maketh a full man."

A universal mark of the called preacher is an insatiable thirst for knowledge, and reading is one sure path to intellectual growth. To those of his men who had no taste for reading, John Wesley said commandingly that they must acquire it! Alexander Whyte, faithful and fruitful Scottish minister, advised, "Sell your shirt and buy books."

(1) THE DISCIPLINED PREACHER HAS READING CENTERS. There is, of course, his private *study room*. Here he houses his books. Everytime he enters his library, the very presence of the volumes creates for him an atmosphere of study and meditation. He loves this room. It is his hideaway—his place of quiet and refuge. Here his great ideas are born and mature.

The very expansiveness of knowledge in the range of books stimulates his mind to new horizons. To enter the room means the freshness of early dawn, the spring green of a landscape, the bracing sea air of an ocean voyage.

It is necessary for the preacher to set aside blocks of time for the study room. The early morning suits some, the late evening is more to the liking of others. Whatever, use the room!

Hopefully the *office* will be a place quite different from his private study room. Interviews, staff meetings, committees, business make up the image of the office. This is, after all, a busy place, what with secretary in and out, callers, the phone ringing.

Yet even this room will not be without its reading matter. The man of God never knows when he will have bits of time. And routine informational materials will come to the office, where he will be more apt to engage in that type of reading.

The *bedstand* will hold magazines, books, and devotional resources. Early morning or late night may provide golden moments of reflection.

The preacher's *traveling briefcase* will, of course, have a magazine or two, books, Bible, a prayer guide. He will allow himself to go nowhere without something to read . . . so also the *glove compartment* of the car will have a periodical or paperback in it; why should he waste the moments while waiting for his wife to complete her shopping?

The wise minister will locate the *libraries* both in his vicinity and in the places to which he travels. Obviously the public library is the first to find; its organization and the quiet corners for reading will soon be discovered. The wise minister will locate, too, the higher education facilities; seminary, college, and university libraries are eager to serve. Courtesy will prompt him to make himself known to appropriate library officials; once his purposes are known, reading, and sometimes borrowing, privileges are offered gladly.

A special word is needed about overseas opportunities. More and more ministers travel, and should there arise the occasion to stay, even a brief time, he would do well to take advantage of a great library. Take only one country as example. Great Britain's book collections rank among the world's best. In London there is the British Museum, repository of every volume, magazine, and pamphlet, map and piece of sheet music printed in the Isles. Comparable to our Library of Congress, it houses a gold mine of material. The National Library of Scotland in Edinburgh is a branch of the British Museum. Dr. Williams' Library of London, not far from the British Museum, makes available a rich storehouse of Puritan and eighteenth-century Evangelical Revival literature. The Friends Library at Euston Station, London, is the depository of Quaker-related riches. The Cambridge University Library possesses holdings of remarkable extent; one of two copyright libraries in England (aside from the British Museum), it has the right to all printed matter in the British Isles free of charge. The Bodleian Library at Oxford shares the honor with Cambridge as England's other copyright library. In Manchester, the John Rylands Library, holder of the famed Rylands Papyrus Fragment of John, stores a vast literature, especially religious. The Biblical section of the Manchester University Library astonishes and delights the eager reader.

Traveling in our own country, one could well afford to take advantage of libraries at Harvard, Yale, Princeton; the Los Angeles Public Library, the New York City Library, and the Library of Congress. One hardly needs mention such a grand facility as the Huntingdon Library, Pasadena, or the vast university libraries, including centers like Urbana, Chicago, Berkeley.

God willing, the day of ministerial sabbaticals universally assured for clergy will soon be a reality. When that great day arrives, the Kingdom cause will reap enormous benefits and devoted ministers themselves will know refreshment, and make new and exciting discoveries in the cloisters of learning.

(2) THE DISCIPLINED MINISTER IS CAREFUL IN HIS SE-

LECTION OF READING MATERIALS. Since we live in a day of
huge quantities of reading matter, the preacher must choose
only the best. That is the ever-present rule of thumb. Seminary training will give him the critical equipment for discerning best, good, and poor.

The reading of the best will constantly suggest more best.
A journal like *The Evangelical Quarterly,* edited by F. F.
Bruce, will carry critical book reviews, guides to superior
volumes in the preacher's fields of interest. Bibliographies of
reputable books constitute a further directive. In the field
of homiletics, the definitive work is Toohey and Thompson,
Recent Homiletical Thought: A Bibliography, 1935-1965.
Omnibus bibliographies furnish assistance to the man building a library. Wilbur M. Smith's *Profitable Bible Study*
(Grand Rapids: Baker, 1963) is a start. The Intervarsity
Fellowship *Guide to Christian Reading* (Revised 1962) suggests by its organization and annotation both the arrangement and quality of a library. Seminary bookstores carry
their own faculty listings, generally bound together in a single
and inexpensive booklet. But in the long run, the minister
will gather around him the writers who contribute most to
his thought life. Some authors—Elton Trueblood, James S.
Stewart, W. E. Sangster—he will discover consistently worthwhile.

The wise preacher will gather about him only quality
books. It is easy to clutter the library with second-rate books,
or volumes of temporary interest and value.

It is wise for the minister to select material for his library
in terms of categories determined by contents.

In the line of *fiction* he will want to have for his own both
classics (Dickens, Hawthorne, George Eliot) and the con-
temporaries (Baldwin, Faulkner, Eudora Welty). In *poetry*
the masters of yesterday (Tennyson, Browning, Keats) will
stimulate him as well as today's poets (Eliot and Auden).
When it comes to *drama* he will see immediately the wisdom
of the bishop who read right through Shakespeare annually
to sharpen his use of language. But he will not exclude

twentieth-century plays which comment eloquently on contemporary society.

Robert J. McCracken, long time minister of Riverside Church, New York, testifies that for him the most helpful kind of reading is *biography*. The minister will do well to absorb himself in the saints and preachers. E. Stanley Jones's *Song of Ascents* is a good beginning point. After that the sky is the limit: Phillips Brooks, Hudson Taylor, Amy Carmichael, David Livingstone. . . . He should not, of course, neglect the men and women who made history: Augustine in Theology, J. S. Bach in music, C. S. Lewis and John Bunyan in literature.

Regular attention must be given to the *news media. Time, Newsweek,* and *U. S. News and World Report* furnish provocative reporting and analyses. *The Manchester Guardian* (available in thin air mail edition), *The Christian Science Monitor, The New York Times, The Los Angeles Times, The Louisville Courier Journal* illustrate careful journalism. Of course, the local press will not be ignored.

Care should be exercised in the choice of *professional journals.* These may well be selected in keeping with individual talents and interests. Not all will appreciate the excellent but somewhat technical materials such as one sees in *New Testament Studies,* the *Journal of Biblical Literature,* or the *Journal of the Evangelical Theological Society.* Some may migrate to papers like *Christianity Today* and *The Expository Times.* The desk of the live and devoted preacher will be well stocked with denominational and popular magazines. Here too the task is to select; after all, there isn't time to read everything. A must is the official organ of the preacher's own denomination—also its official youth, missionary, and other papers. The regular perusal of a first-rate popular sheet such as *Decision* is a good investment of time. In this category the *Reader's Digest* is the standby. This type of reading is next door to recreational. Many a preacher likes detectives; the search-and-seizure theme gears the mind to finding and capturing sermon themes and ideas.

Strange, is it not, how easy it is to forget *theological literature* once out of theological training! Bishop Gerald Ken-
nedy has kept his mind sharp through the years by spending
early morning hours wrestling with the theologians. Match
your wits against the best minds: Thielicke, Temple, Neill;
and men of the past, too: Aquinas, Luther, Wesley.

Quite naturally the preacher will read, hopefully rather
regularly, in the field of *preaching*. Three books cover a large
part of the ground. There is St. Augustine's *Of Christian Doctrine* (Book IV), the first homiletics textbook written and
the whole now available in slender paperback. The second
is Phillips Brooks's Yale Lectures, entitled simply, *Lectures
on Preaching*, now also available in paperback. The last,
James S. Stewart's *Heralds of God* (1945), is without doubt
one of the most exciting books one could read on preaching.

Three lecture series in the homiletical field furnish valuable published material. The Lyman Beecher Lectureship on
Preaching, popularly known as the Yale Lectures, was established in 1871. Batsell B. Baxter's *The Heart of the Yale Lectures* summarizes the preaching principles discussed in the
Yale lectures up to the time of its publication in 1947. The
Warrack Lectures, established 1920, include in addition to
the celebrated Stewart volume mentioned above, H. H. Farmer's *The Servant of the Word* (1942) now available in paperback, and James Black's *The Mystery of Preaching* (1924). A
third lectureship, called the Sprunt Lectures, began in the
academic year 1912-13 at Union Theological Seminary, Richmond. All lectures in this series have not been in the field of
preaching but some have. Examples are G. Campbell Morgan's *The Ministry of the Word* (1914) and the exploratory
The Future Shape of Preaching by Thor Hall (1970).

The preacher who desires to remain qualified for the task
to which he has been called by God, will constantly look for
new books in the preaching field. It is safe to say he cannot
possess too many. It is equally essential that they be selected
rather than merely accumulated.

No more important category is there for the preacher than

tools of interpretation. In addition to Bibles, grammars, and simple concordances, the preacher will secure exhaustive concordances (Young or Strong; Nelson for RSV; Hazard for ASV). Bible dictionaries he will find essential. Among the leaders in this category are the *Interpreter's Dictionary of the Bible* in four volumes edited by George A. Buttrick, a fairly recent set; Hastings' *Dictionary,* revised by F. C. Grant and H. H. Rowley (1963), a one volume tool; and J. D. Douglas' *The New Bible Dictionary* (1962), a wealthy resource. There are a number of Bible atlases from which to choose: Baker Book House did a large atlas by Charles F. Pfeiffer (1961); Wright and Filson's *The Westminster Historical Atlas to the Bible* (Revised 1956) is valuable, especially for its descriptive maps. The smaller Hammond publication, *Atlas of the Bible Lands* (Maplewood, N.J., 1956) is suitable. Rand McNally has produced a paperback.

Theological dictionaries and word books are currently the rage. Kittel's Wörterbuch is appearing in English with translation by G. W. Bromiley under the title, *Theological Dictionary of the New Testament* (Eerdmans), is the leader in its field. *Bible Key Words,* some articles translated from Kittel, is available in several small volumes. Alan Richardson's *A Theological Wordbook of the Bible* (also in paperback) is well known, and the translation of von Allmen's *Vocabulary of the Bible* (London, 1958) is known in America as *A Companion to the Bible* (New York, 1958). William Barclay has done two popular works, *A New Testament Wordbook* (London, 1955) and *More New Testament Words* (London, New York, 1958).

Commentaries, so various in perspective and quality, are indeed difficult to recommend. The preacher might well start with three sets: *The Expositor's Greek Testament* edited by William Robertson Nicoll and reprinted in this country in 1952; William Barclay's *Daily Study Bible,* full of rich homiletical suggestions; and the *Beacon Bible Commentary* (Kansas City, Beacon Press), which includes sermonic suggestions in the running text.

The history of comment is studded with gold nuggets, single volumes of priceless insight. Examples are F. F. Bruce's work on Acts in the *New International Commentary* on the New Testament series (in England called the *New London Commentary*); Sanday and Headlam on Romans in the *International Critical Commentary* series and E. G. Selwyn on I Peter. This List can be expanded by reference to *A Guide to Christian Reading* (A. F. Walls, editor, revised edition, I.V.F., 1962).

Just here underscore an important principle: commentaries ought to be employed only after one's own study of the Scriptural text. Since a commentary is, by its nature, a piece of finished interpretation, the minister who goes to it first robs himself of the chance to think through to his own conclusions under God.

(3) THE DISCIPLINED PREACHER EXERCISES JUDGMENT IN ACQUIRING HIS OWN COLLECTION OF BOOKS.

The building of a library can be a very expensive undertaking. Therefore *the theologian or minister will want to give careful attention to the budgetary aspect of the matter.* First, he does well to discover the used book stores where he can browse, learn, and acquire inexpensively. Second, he will want to purchase *paperbacks* instead of hardbacks whenever possible, when he sees no need for a more permanent binding. Third, he should develop a list of *mail order houses* which deal in used as well as new books. Baker Book House of Grand Rapids, Michigan, operates a huge used book concession. Foyles of London, at 119 Charing Cross Road, W.C.2, runs the largest book concern in the world. Heffers of Cambridge, England (20 Trinity St.) deals extensively in both case bound books and paperbacks. He will make sure that his name gets on the mailing lists of such companies.

If he develops skill at doing acceptable *book reviews,* denominational publishers, magazines, and companies will mail books *gratis,* the preacher's payment for reviewing the book.

Yes, there are ways to "beat the game." But any preacher will have to submit to the discipline of budgeting for books and reading matter if he is to have the necessary money to acquire the books most needed for his instruction and inspiration.

A word of caution should be directed to the preacher who tends to be overly bookish. All theory and no experience makes for an unreal preacher. Ivory towerism, neat and secure, lacks the ring of authenticity. Thus Beecher declared with a wholesome forthrightness: "A man's study should be everywhere—in the house, in the street, in the fields, and in the busy haunts of men."

A word of courage should be directed to the overwhelmed. If the reading program suggested above seems too much, even impossible, remember that you are in process of working out a reading life-style. Except for the unusual man, one cannot read in all the above categories with any kind of regularity. What is important to remember is just this: your library constitutes *a resource;* with discipline tap it as needed.

THE PREACHER'S DESK

John Baillie was a great writer, ever at the business of reducing concepts to writing. Herein is an essential discipline for the minister grappling with ideas and growing in spiritual, social, and intellectual stature. We would suggest the following.

(1) WRITE YOUR SERMONS, WORD FOR WORD, for at least the first two or three years of your ministry. This discipline will fix your preaching style, make you a careful pulpit man, and help develop communication gifts necessary for public work. Arthur John Gossip illustrates the point at hand in a classic way. During the very early years of his ministry, he wrote out his sermons religiously. Then, called up as a chaplain in His Majesty's Forces, he found himself in circumstances thoroughly unsuitable for the careful preparation of manuscripts; he was lucky to make a few notes amid the talk and laughter of the soldiers. But, when he arose to deliver his first sermon to the men, he made a great discovery:

he could make language work effectively on the spot! The years of discipline now bore their fruitage: he could extemporize.

The real work of sermon preparation resides just here. And it is work! The days of the week fill fast with a hundred tasks, often all legitimate, but none more important than learning to communicate. In our American society, in contrast to the British world, we do not learn to put words together in forceful sequence. Expression comes only with great effort. The Britisher has the advantage of home, school, and society employing speech models at a pretty high level; some, of course, live in deprived circumstances, but even they have the BBC with its impeccable English.

We here mention only a few of the excellent books on writing and the use of language. There is Sue Nichols' *Words on Target,* available in paperback. Then there is Rudolf Flesch's *The Art of Readable Writing.* The little pamphlet published by the U. S. Department of Agriculture in Washington, *Writing Words that Work,* supplies first rate guides to written expression. Any preacher would do well to acquire and read these three books.

(2) THE MINISTER IS FACED WITH OTHER WRITING ASSIGNMENTS. Sermons constitute only one writing exercise for the minister. He must take advantage of every opportunity to improve his skill and to witness in print. In this connection he should not forget that part of that witness is the witness of excellence. Accordingly, he will seek to produce a letter-perfect bulletin, a parish paper of carefully honed English, and faithfully executed advertisements and articles for the local press. Proof-reading must be a lifelong habit, a rule that in our society needs underscoring.

"Most ministers," says *Decision's* editor, Sherwood Wirt, "have no idea of the potential of evangelistic literature" (*Baker's Dictionary of Practical Theology,* Ralph G. Turnbull, ed., 1967, p. 309). This is quite true; but if the preacher sees the potential of written communication of the gospel, he will be ever at the business. He will keep something on the back burner continuously, and he will be ever on the alert for an opportune time to serve it. This may be an article for the denominational organ, a letter to the editor of the local press, or a book of worthy sermons. Let's face it, literature is one of God's chosen means of propagating His truth.

THE PREACHER'S ALTAR

Faithfully and daily John Baillie knelt at the little home altar and prayer desk in his study. There he made his daily sacrifice of praise. Baillie learned that prayer and the cultivation of the human spirit are absolutely essential. The development of one's interior resources determines the shape of one's exterior reactions.

We here submit a devotional pattern which has proved effective in the lives of many devoted servants of God:

• Start the day with the Bible. Begin with the Psalms, for they bring together prayer and praise. Bishop Stephen Neill says the best way to learn to pray is to read the Psalms. He observes that *The Book of Common Prayer* divides the Psalms into daily readings to cover a monthly cycle. To begin the day with Psalms is to begin it with God.

• Follow reading from the Psalms with a chapter in Proverbs, the world's greatest repository of wisdom. Billy Graham has made it a lifetime discipline to read, first thing in the morning, five Psalms to get into right relatedness with God, and one chapter from Proverbs to right his relationships with man.

• Then, read in a devotional guide, such as E. Stanley Jones' *Abundant Living,* thus stimulating and stretching mind and heart.

• Next, give yourself to prayer. Praise must be the *alpha* and *omega* of the experience, and intercession must take precedence over petition (prayer for yourself). Develop a prayer journal, a small pocket notebook: on left pages place names and concerns, on right pages record answers. This procedure is especially useful during one's early years while he is learning that God does in fact answer prayer. Eventually one will say with Arnold Prater, "There are some things I no longer doubt—one of them is the validity of intercessory prayer."

W. E. Sangster recommended fifteen minutes in the morning and ten at night for beginners. Ministers, to be effective, will go beyond the beginner stage, and develop a rich and varied life of devotion. Unfortunately, some do not engage in any regular and systematic devotional program, much less in the development of a life that, with the apostle Paul, prays "without ceasing." One who does not have a specific time of prayer is not likely to live that life of ceaseless devotion.

The prayerful life is a fruitful life. If argumentation is needed for prayer, listen to E. Stanley Jones, master of the art of devotion and saint of the twentieth century. "I find by actual experience I am better or worse as I pray more or less. If my prayer life sags, my whole life sags with it; if my prayer life goes up, my life as a whole goes up with it. To fail here is to fail all down the line; to succeed here is to succeed everywhere" (Quoted in Eunice Jones Matthews and James K. Matthews, *Selections from E. Stanley Jones, Christ and Human Need,* p. 133). This is why Martin Luther could say that he who prays well works well.

Listen once more, this time to William Penn speaking of his close friend, George Fox. He excelled in prayer "above all," declared Penn. "The inwardness and weight of his spirit, the reverence and solemnity of his address and behaviour, and the fewness and fulness of his words, have often struck, even strangers, with admiration, as they used to reach others with consolation. The most awful, living, reverent frame I ever felt or beheld, I must say was his in prayer. And truly it was a testimony he knew and lived nearer to the Lord than other men; for they that know him most will see most reason to approach him with reverence and fear" (from the Preface of the 1694 [first] edition of Fox's *Journal*).

In these testimonies we see illustrated a fundamental principle for the preacher. The spiritually developed man knows that powerful and effective sermons come through prayer. True preaching is God talking through His prophet; neat essays in themselves are not God disclosing Himself, nor are entertaining talks. Why, according to tradition, was James the brother of Jesus called "camel-kneed"? It is said that he wore callouses on his knees from much praying; no wonder he was God's spokesman.* What was the secret of John Wesley's great preaching and organizational power? He had an excellent and disciplined mind, yes; he was master of the English language, ever employing mouth and pen to useful purpose. But his hour of prayer and devotion each morning, and again each evening, made him the effective servant of God which history says he was.

A young minister did not really believe in "this prayer business," but in all honesty determined to give it a try. Every morning found him thirty minutes at the altar of his church. And by the close of those minutes he found his memo pad filled with God's assignments for the day. He was beginning to learn that prayer is a two-way street. He spoke to God— but God also spoke to him. He discovered the inestimable value not only of speaking to God, but also of listening to God.

The formulation of gospel concepts accurately, succinctly, and communicatively should be regarded as the fruit of prayer. The truly devoted preacher recognizes that. Ideas and their shape come from God and are an answer to prayer. The minister is deeply conscious of the fact that time, openness, a spirit of leisure and receptivity are the requirements for a meaningful and fruitful kind of prayer involvement. This recognition is the fruit of consistent prayer discipline through the years. Faster than he may expect, the preacher

---

*"According to Hegesippus, writing ca. 180 (quoted by Eusebius, Hist. II. 23.4-18), James was a Nazarite and spent so much time on his knees in intercession for the people that his knees grew horny like a camel's" (*Interpreter's Dictionary of the Bible*. Nashville: Abingdon, Vol. E-J, p. 793).

prepares his sermons in the spirit of prayer, and the happy fruit is the feeding of God's people on the very bread of life.

THE PREACHER'S RECREATIONAL LIFE

We come now to the fourth discipline, relaxation. Recreation, if it is to serve its purpose, requires discipline, including careful scheduling. Here may be the weakest link in the modern preacher's chain of disciplines.

Many a man is convinced that he cannot take a day off. Such indiscipline can easily result in a three-way tragedy: for the church or organization for which he works, for his family, for himself: (1) for the church or organization, because he will not bring to his preaching task and responsibilities a freshness and vigor required to function at optimum level; (2) for his family, because they will feel he does not have time to be a good husband and father, to have a good time, and temporarily to forget everything connected with his professional existence; (3) for himself, because the constant strain and stress may mean that sooner or later he will have to take forced rest.

The young minister needs to realize he is not called upon to do everything, and that God is the true Governor of the affairs of men. The man who simply will not accept this basic theological fact and act upon it, will probably have to drop out of the ministry. America is filled with ex-clergymen.

The minister, of all people, needs to throw his head back and laugh heartily now and then. Recent medical research demonstrates that laughter affects every organ of the body—to the good! Laughter and release of spirit make the minister a contagious, open channel of communication, and demonstrate the joy of the Lord.

Even as there can be a rule for daily devotion, so there can be for recreation. Some such pattern as this will work:

- Write into desk and pocket calendars your days off: the football game with your son, the picnic with the family, etc. *Keep these dates religiously.*

- John Stott has both a day off, and a planning day in the country where he is unavailable. (That helps explain his pulpit effectiveness!) Such a plan may be talked out with your board so that there is mutual understanding of an established pattern.

- Get the sleep you require. Requirements differ, but the average is 7½ to 8 hours. Rare is the person, like Albert Schweitzer, who can exist normally on five hours.

- Develop hobbies: gardening, stamp collecting, coins, painting, whatever. Hobbies must be diverting and challenging to do their job.

- Regiment yourself to some regular exercise: swimming, jogging, tennis, golf—something.

- Lead your church or organization in recreation. Let your people know, in your own way, that fun and recreation are good gifts of God. Go with your teens to the ball games, participate in the church picnics, join the men at the football stadium—anything to communicate your full enjoyment of life.

THE PREACHER'S LISTENING EAR

John Baillie, like any successful man in the professions, learned to listen. Listening is difficult for the average minister, for he is trained to talk more than listen!

There are several ways of listening:

- *The cassette.* Word, Inc. has made available one of the first knowledge banks for the preacher. Subscribed to just as you would a magazine, it plays in car, office, or home. Its assigned task is summarizing the best from religious journals and resources, keeping the minister abreast of the times.

- *Tape and record.* Sermons and other relevant materials are obtained easily, and advertisements will come to your desk periodically.

- *Television and radio.* Despite the generally inferior level of broadcasting, these media provide the richest sources of worldwide information both cultural and factual. Attention can mean awareness on the wavelength of people everywhere.

• *People.* People are your most important source of information! Listen to discover thought currents, church and ecclesiastical movements, individual hang-ups. Inevitably such listening affects preaching and the shape of one's ministry.

There is *a time to quit listening.* Listening is hard work if done creatively. Actually, quite a lot of the minister's job requires a listening ear, more than the average person. Normally, a person spends 45 percent of his communication time listening. Dr. Paul Rankin of Ohio State University, learned that the average person spends 70 percent of his waking hours in communication: 9 percent writing, 16 percent reading, 30 percent speaking, and 45 percent listening—the largest percentage. Because listening means the consuming of time and energy, the man of God knows when he should quit listening to restore his own resources. After all, the next round of listening on phone, in committee, and interview is just around the corner.

PART TWO:
THE SERMON

III. THE SEARCH AND SEIZURE OF SUBJECTS, PLANNING, AND STORING

John Wesley, keen on discipline, rightly underscored it for his preachers. Said he in a typical statement, "Wisely said the ancients, 'The soul and body make a man; the Spirit and discipline make a Christian.' "

A sure mark of the disciplined preacher, in Wesley's day or ours, is the calculated organization of his efforts in the finding and fixing of sermonic themes, with supporting materials. This fundamentally significant subject constitutes the thrust of this chapter.

THE PRIMARY SECRET OF FINDING THEMES

The steady employment of the Bible is the first secret. The Bible must ever play its role as preacher's textbook; when something else plays that supreme role, the preacher sooner or later, but inevitably, runs out of meaningful topics and materials for preaching.

(1) SATURATION IN THE SCRIPTURES. The first book the preacher reads in the morning, and the last at night, is the Bible. Devotional guides—the *Book of Common Prayer* is classic—must be Bible oriented. The pattern for daily devotions suggested in the preceding chapter is not the only one which can be followed. Elton Trueblood reads the Gospels at breakfast, morning by morning, marking his way through them. A daily discipline with him, the mark tells him where he has actually read—no guessing! Herein lies part of the secret of that man's remarkable productivity as preacher, and writer on Biblical themes.

And this can be the secret of your productivity and effec-

tiveness too! Do anything and everything to make the Bible
yours. Read, mark, underline, write in the margins; do it
daily. Set aside chunks of time for special attention to the
Scriptures, for word study and commentary guidance. Employ devotional interpretations such as William Temple's
Readings in St. John's Gospel, James S. Stewart's *The Life
and Teaching of Jesus,* and William Barclay's *The Master's Men.* The precise pattern of Bible exposure is not the
issue at stake; the issue is the preacher's actual saturation in
the Scriptures so that they become part of him and his life-
style.

Saturation—that is the first step to acquiring Bible themes
for preaching.

(2) PREACHING FROM THE SCRIPTURES. D. Martyn Lloyd-
Jones advised a seminary professor in these words: "Tell
your young men at the seminary to preach the Bible." One
would expect that from the great expositor; one would also
expect what he said next: "Yes, tell them to preach the
Bible, and that if they do they will have more texts they
want to expound than opportunities to preach."

How true this statement! The preacher-thinker discovers
sooner or later—sooner it is hoped—that the great function
of the Bible is to reveal life. It opens our minds to the laws
by which we discover God, ourselves, and others in fulfilling
relationships. Its distilled truth about real life and meaning
makes it the most exciting discovery book in the world; this
accounts for its contagion. Preach the Bible, and the truth
that makes people free becomes increasingly and marvelously
vivid. In that frame of reference one can scarcely wait for
the next opportunity to lift from it some new and glittering
nugget.

Gordon W. Allport in his monumental work, *Personality,*
isolates a law of human behavior he calls "functional autonomy." A young boy goes to sea, not particularly inclined to
sailing, but necessity demands that he go. With the passage
of the years he absorbs the sea and its magic ways; it takes
on a beauty that draws him and he is "caught." Though he

now receives an offer of employment on land, perhaps the very job he had dreamed of in previous years, he refuses, for now the sea is in him. He must go back to sea. The poet Masefield sang, "I must go back to the sea again"; but that is only mild nostalgia—haunting to be sure, but passing. No, the boy *must* go back to the sea and make his living just there. The law of functional autonomy has come to full flower. Ships and sailing, rigs and rigging project a permanent image on the very soul of the man. Not a mere fever—a fever passes —the sea is now a fervor.

Live with the Bible until it lives in you. Preach it consistently, even in your early years when the going is just plain hard. Then some day it will become "functionally autonomous" and you will find yourself in the happily awkward situation of having fewer opportunities to preach than you have texts from which to preach.

AN INDISPENSABLE CHARACTERISTIC: DECISIVENESS

The Biblically saturated preacher finds himself confronted with a real and regular problem. In the great range of possibilities, what specific subject and text will he choose? The needs of the people and the Inner Voice will, of course, be heeded with care. But there are many texts which on any given occasion might be admirably suited to meet specific needs. Contemplating these numerous possibilities may easily result in the waste of a good deal of time.

The point is this: don't fritter away time deciding. Decide. Pray openly, sensitively, sincerely. Believe, by sheer act of the will if necessary, that God Himself will guide you to *His* text for *His* occasion. Then, once located, seize the text and keep it tenaciously.

One poor man habitually thinks—Saturday night of all times!—that he has chosen the wrong text. Often he stays up half of Saturday night preparing a fresh sermon.

Decisiveness is a character trait imperative to every minister. Some have also said that it is the best tranquilizer.

DEVELOP A PLANNING GUIDE

Were Wesley alive today, surely he would insist that a significant part of the discipline he insisted upon must be planning ahead. He planned for the future in every way; he would require men to map out a program of preaching designed to meet the needs of specific tasks and local situations.

(1) ESSENTIAL TO THE MINISTER'S WORK IS THE PLANNING GUIDE. This is true for at least two reasons. First, the yearly plan guides and directs the selection of themes. How much easier to decide if the preacher has a series of ready-made slots into which he may drop texts when they come to mind. He will soon discover a number of Sundays set aside for special purposes and occasions by the denominational calendar sent to him from headquarters. He will fill in many of the remaining Sundays with a view to the specific needs of his people, the observance of holidays, and the commemoration of special events. In this way the task of specific text-finding is simplified.

A second reason for the importance of a long-term planning guide is the need for providing a balanced spiritual diet for those whom God has entrusted to his care. The preacher is professionally obliged to provide balanced, well-rounded fare. The Episcopal (Anglican) Church has a built-in guarantee in the Biblical and doctrinal completeness of the *Prayer Book*. The Lutheran communions do the same with a pericope system (cf. Paul W. Nesper, *Biblical Texts*). But the free churches throw the burden of responsibility for balanced planning on the ministers themselves. Unfortunately, more frequently than not, large chunks of Christian truth are quite foreign to free church people because the minister refuses to trouble himself with the task or does not know how to go about it.

This is a serious matter. An unbalanced diet accounts in no small measure for doctrinal error, moral failure, and spiritual sickness. God's people must be thoroughly grounded and built up (Paul uses the term "edified") in the faith. The planning guide to preaching is an obvious aid for the preacher toward doing his God-centered work.

(2) EXAMPLES OF PLANNING PROGRAMS. The guides employed by two seasoned ministers of the gospel are here discussed from information provided by *Christianity Today's* paperback, *How to Prepare and Deliver Better Sermons*. The first man, C. Ralston Smith, divides his year like this:

Labor Day to Thanksgiving
Advent
New Year's Day to Lent
Lent to Easter
Easter to Pentecost
The Summer Months

Within such a workable framework it is fairly simple to cover the grand themes of Bible truth, and to plan for the great days of celebration in the Christian year.

Richard C. Halverson, Presbyterian pastor of Washington, D. C., follows this plan:

FALL QUARTER
(October to Christmas)

The Anticipation of Christ's Advent
(Old Testament Emphasis)

WINTER QUARTER
(January to Easter)

The Life of Christ
(Emphasis on the Gospels)

SPRING QUARTER
(Easter through June)

The Church
(Emphasis on Acts or the Epistles)

SUMMER QUARTER
(July to Fall)

Special Series, Sometimes Topical
("Needed to create a balanced spiritual diet")

In his planning Halverson is guided by his philosophy of Biblical preaching, which he expresses as follows, "I make a deliberate effort not to over-emphasize certain portions of Scripture to the neglect of others, and to preach from every book in the Bible at some time during a period of three to five years. Sunday evening messages are generally book-by-book or verse-by-verse studies. Most of my messages are expository, with the theme, content, outline, and topic coming from the Scripture passage under consideration."

Very helpfully, Pastor Halverson goes on to share with us examples of sermon themes in the framework of a quarterly plan.

Fall quarter with emphasis on Old Testament preaching:

Example 1: A biographical series, "The Patriarchs and the Prophets."
Example 2: A series on "Christ in the Old Testament."
Example 3: "Famous Psalms."

Winter quarter with emphasis on preaching from the Gospels:

Example 1: Preaching through Luke.
Example 2: Series entitled, "Great Events in the Life of Our Lord."
Example 3: A sequence on "The Person and Work of Christ."
Example 4: A series of sermons called, "A Harmony of the Gospels."
Example 5: Series named, "The Disciples of Jesus."
Example 6: A series on "People Jesus Helped."

Spring quarter with emphasis on doctrinal themes from Acts and the Epistles:

Example 1: Series entitled, "Outline of Reformed Doctrine."
Example 2: Another doctrinal series: "The Apostles Creed."
Example 3: Another: "The Westminster Confession of Faith."

(Make your own . . . like these: "The Articles of Religion"; "The Doctrine of the Holy Spirit"; "Contemporary Doctrinal Creeds.")

Dr. Halverson gives still further help by sharing Sunday evening planning. One series explored the Minor Prophets, one book per week. Another extended over a six month period and included Mark, James, I Peter, Ephesians, I John, and some of Revelation. "Exploits of Faith," a sequence on the men and women of Hebrews 11, related each person to his full background in the Old Testament. A final example was "The Ethics of the Apostles."

The genius of this kind of preaching is that it comes to grips with the great problems of human life with the authority of the Scriptures themselves. That is precisely why Dr. Halverson says he has drawn "my sermons from the Scriptures rather than to attempt to contrive relevance by addressing myself to current issues. In the providence of God, rarely does a passage, planned months before, fail to meet the people at the point of present need." When one stops to remember that Dr. Halverson ministers in Washington, where the relevance of the gospel to crucial issues is sorely needed, his testimony takes on all the greater significance.

(3) WHEN WILL THE OUTLINED PLANNING GUIDE BE DONE? One preacher has his fairly well in hand by Labor Day. That would appear to be a pretty sensible target date. Summer is over, children retrace their steps to the schools, young adults return to university, business and social calendars take on new life. Why not have the preaching calendar in hand at this time of new or resumed activity?

Another man captures a general purview of his church year, but determines his specific sermon plans quarter by quarter. He prints topics on slip covers put over hymnbooks at the outset of each three month period. Such a plan commends itself by its manageable divisions. Its risk is in the temptation to work through quarters only, virtually ignoring the

scope of the total year. But the same caution may well be regarded by the one who works only year by year, giving
little or no attention to the larger three to five year block.
Somehow Biblical, doctrinal, and ethical coverage needs to
be given consideration and then nailed down.

This is all very well in theory. The question now comes,
How does one get to the actual business of pencil-and-paper
specificity? One minister takes a note pad with him as he
rows to the middle of his summer vacation lake. This he does
on two or three consecutive days, until the year's planning
falls into place completely and satisfactorily. Some will criti-
cize this procedure on the basis that during holiday periods
the preacher should "forget it all." The point is that some
period or periods must be set aside for prayerful and careful
planning. The preacher must decide, in the earliest years of
his ministry, the time, place, and working life-style most
suitable to him for those preparation periods. Sad to say,
some never come around to such planning-ahead at all. They
are not the only losers. The people entrusted to their care
are certain to suffer from a meager and unbalanced spiritual
diet.

(4) THE HOMILETICAL GARDEN. The homiletical garden
concept originated with Andrew W. Blackwood, late professor of preaching at Princeton Theological Seminary. Says
Richard C. Halverson, who grows his garden religiously, "Dr.
Blackwood's practical concept of the 'homiletical garden' in
which one plants sermonic seeds and allows them to grow
without interference but with proper nourishment, liberated
me from a fearful question that beset me in seminary—name-
ly, How is it possible to produce two new sermons every
week year after year together with Bible studies for midweek
services and occasional special talks? Actually, it has turned
out as Dr. Blackwood predicted; the problem is not having
something to preach but having opportunity enough to preach
the messages that demand expression" (*How to Prepare and
Deliver Better Sermons,* p. 11).

Halverson grows his garden this way: Each year he purchases a common daybook, and sets aside one page per preaching day. Each page has its date, sermon theme or topics, sermonic data, Scriptural references. Six pages are left at the back for cross-referencing, illustrations, hymns, and other relevant matter. Testifies this seasoned garden grower: "It is surprising how the garden grows. Often the sermons seem almost to prepare themselves."

Another man's garden is grown quite differently but with the same results. An envelope for each sermon of the year is marked with date, topic, text (one could add occasion— e.g., Mother's Day). Clippings and notes are deposited in the envelopes as materials and ideas come forward from reading and other sources of stimulation. Envelopes are easy to file simply and manageably by date. When sermon construction time comes, the contents of the envelope filed under next Sunday's date, are arranged on a table. The problem for the preacher is not in having enough material, but determining which materials best suit the sermon—a good problem.

However one shapes the actual homiletical garden, the genius of the concept itself lies in just this: *When time comes to put together the sermon or address for the next speaking event, materials are at hand.* How can anyone improve on that?

THE PREACHING BANK ACCOUNTS

There is a larger homiletical garden that needs cultivating. But it is better to change the figure of speech at this point. There are preaching bank accounts into which deposits over the years will bring excellent returns.

(1) BANKING ACCOUNT NO. 1: SERMON IDEAS. Deposit ideas on 4 x 6 inch cards or sheets. Backs of bond paper letters cut to size will save considerable amounts of money over the years, and also take up less space than cards. File alphabetically by category. A typical card could follow a format rather much like this:

CATEGORY:_____

Subject or Topic:_____

Scripture References: _____

Possible Outline:_____

_____

_____

_____

Illustrations in Embryo:_____

_____

_____

Resources:_____

_____

_____

Let your cards develop as you read and warm to ideas. Often several, even all, blank lines on the card fill in quickly. Inspired moments are sometimes richly fruitful.

Here are examples of seed thoughts which could flower into eleven 4 x 6 cards with suggestions for as many sermons to be preached when the occasion seems appropriate.

CATEGORY: Great Questions of the Bible
Scripture References: Matthew 16:26
                        Genesis 4:9
                        Romans 8:31
                        John 18:38
                        Ecclesiastes 1:3
                        Luke 10:25
CATEGORY: Great 3:16 verses in the Bible
Scripture References: John 3:16
                        I John 3:16
                        Ephesians 3:16
                        II Timothy 3:16
                        James 3:16

Actually, years may pass before a sermon suggested by a card in the minister's bank account is preached. In fact, some sermon seeds never come to flower; but time is never wasted. The preacher is learning to think homiletically, and with the making of each new card he adds to his own memory bank that which may come to his rescue at the most advantageous and unexpected times. Besides, ideas kept on slow heat are more likely to come to the point when they can be placed before the people in a palatable and digestible form.

Earlier and in passing, reference was made to a partial but, insofar as it is complete, ready-made bank account. Nesper's *Biblical Texts* (Minneapolis: 1932), is a volume which ranges through the Scriptures presenting texts arranged under special days and categories. It can be of great help to the minister in two ways. It can assist him in planning a program and by suggesting texts for particular days and occasions.

Another ready-made account, but of a very different nature, is Hastings's *The Speaker's Bible*. This set contains sermon substance in summary form from master preachers on both Old and New Testament texts. The multivolume work is priceless when used with discretion. Any preacher must be careful not to imitate or quote language or to use illustrations out of character with his own culture, national and local, and his own time. The space age requires a posture quite different from that of the past.

Other sermon materials and idea banks there are a plenty—some useful, some merely collections of outmoded currency. In the last analysis, the preacher's own bank of ideas will prove most useful. These ideas have passed through his own mind and will carry emotional and intellectual excitement which borrowed thoughts cannot possibly carry.

Aside from all this, the building of this bank of ideas is an inspiring, constructive, maturing activity which will pay rich dividends for the preacher and those whom he is called to serve.

(2) BANKING ACCOUNT NO. 2: QUOTATIONS AND ILLUSTRATIONS. When you run across striking quotations and illustrations, write or type them out on 4 x 6 cards. Do not hesitate to snatch a card and write in long hand when a

typewriter is not readily available. Some such format as this may be used.

CATEGORY: (e.g., Sin)
Quotation:

Source:

The source should be clearly indicated. It may be a book, in which case the author, title, publisher, date, and page should be noted. In case of a lecture or sermon, the occasion, speaker, and title of the lecture or sermon topic should be given.

You may wish to begin by filing your card collection in a shoe box. The cards should be arranged alphabetically according to category. Later you may wish to buy a heavy cardboard box for 4 x 6 filing; eventually, you will want a permanent wood or steel box, an essential for the safekeeping of materials that represent, by this time, two or three years' investment.

Two or three suggestions may prove helpful for the development of the 4 x 6 quotation and illustration file. (a) A preacher should carry a few of these cards with him in an inside coat pocket or in his wallet. A man like Elton Trueblood does this out of habit: he is never without them. The result is that he always has access to fresh ideas in black and white, ideas from which he draws for making sermons and books. It is important to file the cards at the first opportunity lest they be misplaced, forgotten, lost, or unwittingly discarded.

(b) Much time can be saved if when reading you simply underline the quotations for copying, and write an F (for Filing) in the margin. Then your reading will not be interrupted. You can go back to the book and write or type the quotation or illustration on the filing card. You can also have someone else do this for you.

(c) Snippets can be glued or taped to 4 x 6 cards. For

example, a small piece from *Time* magazine can be quickly cut out and glued onto a card. It is important that bibliographic data be properly recorded for future information.

Try to keep things simple. You may wish to purchase a small notebook in which you can enter cross-references to the cards in your file box. The same can be accomplished by adding cards on which you enter cross-references. For example:

Music. See:
Bach
Hymns
Piano

The important point is: *Organize file so as to locate quickly.*

(3) BANKING ACCOUNT NO. 3: THE PREACHER'S 9 x 12 TOPICAL FILE. The development of an illustration and human interest file of 9 x 12 folders may prove useful beyond expectations. The file should be allowed to expand without any effort at restriction. Paul Rees developed such a file with literally thousands of items in it; the richness of his preaching is proof of its value for him.

A word needs to be said about development of captions and categories under which to file. The principle outlined actually applies to all sermonic filing. Ready-made filing programs, with preprogrammed subject- and subheads are readily available. Notebooks and instruction manuals, in fact fully organized schemes, are obtainable. But there are difficulties. They were prepared for the general use of preachers and may not suit your taste and needs. Large, bulky filing schemes also tend to fall under their own weight. Because of their mass and complexity they may not fit your size. A good rule is: *Avoid complexity; employ simplicity.*

Other rules of thumb can be reviewed quickly. Begin humbly, starting with as little expense as possible. Keep expansion ever in mind; anything that confines future growth cramps one's style. Let seasoning in the work of the ministry dictate the larger equipment you purchase; buying heavy, expensive filing equipment and filing furniture too soon can prove wasteful. If confusion seems to capture you at first, be patient; you and your filing system will develop together. And if you feel you must have some initial guidance on captions for organizing your files, you may receive help from A. W. Blackwood's simple beginning list:

Art and Architecture	Ministry (The)
Baptism	Miracles
Bible	Missions
Biography (non-Biblical)	Money
Characters—O.T.	Nation
Characters—N.T.	Parables—Matthew
Children	Parables—Luke
Christ—Birth (Christmas)	Poems
Christ—Character	Prayer
Christ—Life	Prophets
Christ—Teachings	Providence
Christ—Death	Psalms
Christ—Resurrection	Sabbath
Christ—Second Coming	Sabbath school
Church	Sermon on the Mount
Christian Life (subdivide)	Service
Conscience	Sin
Conversion	Special Days (subdivide)
Education	Temperance
Evangelism	Temptation
Faith (and Doubt)	Ten Commandments
Forgiveness	Theology (subdivide later)
Friendship	Vices
Funeral	Virtues
God	War (and Peace)
Heaven	Woman
Holy Spirit	Work
Hymns (and Music)	Worry
Lord's Supper	Young People
Love	

Any preacher electing to use these captions as a start should immediately add headings reflecting today's wavelength: Space, Transportation, Communications, etc. He should avoid yielding to the temptation of adding too many categories at the outset. It is better to add these as the file expands, as items and clippings of interest are found.

He may wish to explore other possibilities for cataloging. For example, there is the Dewey system of classification. In the field of religion, two systems are available. *Expansion of Dewey 200* by Clara B. Allen, may be obtained by addressing the Librarians' Cooperative, 4809 North Armel Drive, Covina, California 91722. *Dewey Decimal Classification (200 Religion Class)* may be purchased through the Broadman Press, 127 Ninth Avenue North, Nashville, Tennessee 37203. Some have organized their entire libraries and filing systems under such a unified system. A preacher is well advised, however, not to start an ambitious program unless his interests have the capacity to sustain what he begins. It is practically essential to have clerical assistance in order to operate at the near-professional level indicated by the systems mentioned.

In short, discover for yourself the filing system that saves time and suits your purpose.

(4) BANKING ACCOUNT NO. 4: SERMONS PREACHED. George Arthur Buttrick's wife has filed his sermons for years, and keeps them intact with the care she would handle gold bullion. Harold J. Ockenga files all addresses; this provides him records of what he has preached and when. As a general rule, never throw a sermon away. File it to provide necessary information: topics, texts, dates, places. Don't be caught in the embarrassing position of the minister who preached the same Mother's Day sermon three years straight to the same congregation!

The values of filing your sermons, however, go way beyond "saving face," even beyond the guarantee of fresh and well rounded fare. With the passage of the years, those files may prove pure gold. There you may find substance capable of reshaping for publication: in a book, in your church organ, for a position paper at a church or social-action conference. Again, you may have done a series of sermons with better-than-average response, and these you will want to share with a wider public: xeroxed for your people to buy (at 25 or 30 cents) and give away; delivered at a preaching mission in another part of the country.

Save your sermons. Don't be caught at some point down the road of the future with the sigh, "Oh, if I had only kept *that!*" or "I know it's here . . . if I could only put my finger on it!"

Filing the past is one way of planning for the future.

Now, how do we go about the business of filing the sermon scripts?

(a) Organize the master sermon file by date and Sunday, like this:

Sunday, May 13, 1973. MOTHER'S DAY.

Sunday, May 20, 1973. ARMED FORCES DAY.

Sunday, May 27, 1973. SERIES: "Preparing for
Summer and Leisure" (1)

(b) For sermons preached in other churches, organize a separate file like this:

FIRST CHURCH, SEATTLE

ST. PAUL'S, LEXINGTON

JOHN PAUL MEMORIAL, DURHAM

On each sermon, record:

Scripture Reading

Text

Topic

Place

Church Name

Time of Service

Setting (Worship, Youth Group, etc.)

(c) With the passage of time, you may feel the need of developing a topical card index. Use either 3 x 5 or 4 x 6 cards, like this:

SALVATION

1. See Sunday, December 17, 1972.

2. See Sunday, June 11, 1972.

Let it grow over the years.

(d) File manuscripts and attach to the sermon notes you used in the pulpit. Throw jottings and drafts away, but not these two items.

IV. THE MARKS OF A GOOD INTRODUCTION

It is hardly an exaggeration to say that no well-turned introduction comes off the lathe without hard work and fervent prayer.

Why is the introduction so important? Simply this: in the first two minutes you have your congregation or you don't. In those first moments the stage is set and the mood fixed. Actually, as someone has rightly said, the very *first sentence* sounds a note not easily changed.

WHY INTRODUCTIONS?

Perhaps no rhetorician has improved on Cicero's three answers: (1) to arouse interest, (2) to secure favor, and (3) to prepare to lead.

(1) To AROUSE INTEREST involves, among other things, a carefully wrought first sentence. In preparing this first sentence: mull it over in your mind; frame it on paper; reframe it; revise it as many times as necessary. Perfect it for interest and clarity.

But the whole of the introduction must arouse interest. It is during those first two or more minutes that people make a decision of high importance—whether or not to listen to the gospel on this particular occasion.

Someone has said there are three kinds of preachers: those you cannot listen to, those you can listen to, and those you must listen to. People do not generally come to church with the first alternative in the backs of their minds. Either they come with the intention to listen or they just do not come. But most probably option two *is* their orientation. The

67

preacher's task in those first few moments is to persuade them to opt for number three.

Arouse interest.

(2) To SECURE FAVOR is related to, but quite distinct from, arousing interest. The task here is to win goodwill and to make real the meeting of minds between preacher and people.

This task differs according to the setting. Suppose the preacher addresses a strange audience. One way to orient himself as well as his message may be by the use of humor. The result of such a response is the providing of a context of ease for the speaker and the opening of the door to listening. This is exactly what happened when Paul Rees, after a long and highly complimentary introduction, replied: "I have two reactions: First, I know I shouldn't have heard that; but I'm awfully glad Mrs. Rees was here to hear it."

That was Dr. Rees's beginning comment in the first address of a ministers' conference series; at the outset of his second talk no such remarks were needed, and the preliminaries were wisely omitted. He got down to business right off, what people, after all, really wanted at this point. Audiences like to laugh, but their purpose is not entertainment; people want assurance that something worthwhile will be said. When humor is considered necessary and therapeutic, have it; when unnecessary, refrain!

In getting down to business, there must be projected by the speaker an attractiveness. What constitutes attractiveness is not always easily determined. We do know that friendliness and warmth are essential. They say, "Your preacher wants to help you; he is open to your needs; more than anything he desires to be the instrument of God's authentic Word." Closely associated with warm friendliness is genuine spirituality. People sense in a minute when the preacher has been with and learned of God. They seem to recognize almost instinctively the godly man who can help them.

The day of starchy oratory is past. Living-room conversation is the medium of sermon delivery today. It attracts; it puts people at ease. It says both verbally and nonverbally,

"You are in my circle of confidence, and you are there because I like you and am concerned."

(3) The third purpose of the introduction as stated by Cicero, is to PREPARE TO LEAD. The secret of pulpit leadership is captured in three words: *orientation, initiative, purpose.*

People will not be led if they are not ready to be led. Orientation grapples with that specific need. Its task is to bring the people from the busyness of their manifold concerns to the business of divine concerns; indeed, its aim is to bring their very busyness to the feet of God. Actually, this is what they want; but they need help achieving the transfer of thought.

This indicates why the planning of the entire service around a single goal is important. There is actually an introduction before the sermon introduction. The preparation of the very atmosphere for the sermon's beginning words is extremely important. Hymns, prayers, and Bible reading should be carefully planned with the sermon in view. This will assist greatly the delivery of God's Word.

To orient means to face the east, the rising sun; it is to get the day started. It is at once imperative and beautifully fruitful to achieve the great task of turning your people Godward, pointing them in the direction of a specific truth to be presented in sermon form.

To do this effectively the minister himself must take the initiative. He cannot depend on his platform associates, as sensitive as he hopes they will be to the tone of the service. He is in charge of the service; he is the director. His very demeanor says, without officiousness, "Under God, I am in charge." Whether reading his call to worship or projecting the first sentence of the sermon, the preacher's initiative must be one thing which is absolutely clear.

To no small degree, this projected sense of initiative gives psychological shape to the first sentence and introduction of the sermon. It speaks of purpose. Even as one can tell instantly if a man, walking through a busy city street, knows

where he is going by the character and purposiveness of his
step, so an audience senses the sure step of the preacher in
his first lines. He will lead his people in the unfolding of the
Word of God only if they feel assured that he knows where
he is going.

HOW INTRODUCTIONS?

We have discussed the *why* of introductions. We must now
come to grips with the *how* of introductions. We will discuss
seven methods of making beginning statements. It is important
to remember that not one of them is mutually exclusive, since
techniques often combine or overlap in one way or another.

(1)First there is the time-honored TEXTUAL METHOD. Ancient though it is, the simple announcement of the text at the
outset constitutes one effective way to begin. "This morning
my text reads. . . ."

Employ this method, and use it more or less frequently,
but with certain precautions clearly in mind. Do not allow
it to breed contempt by using hackneyed phrases and worn
out ideas. The best way to avoid this homiletical "blooper"
is to relate the text to the contemporary situation, thus rendering it thoroughly relevant and vibrantly alive.

Here in skeletal and incomplete format, is one way of
using this type of introduction.

Begin this way:

> Today marks the first in a preaching series—
> "Great Words of the Bible."
> Three words will capture our attention:
> Wait—is the word for next Sunday.
> Go—that is for the third Sunday.
> Come—is our word for today.

You have now created a mood of anticipation. Without
further comment on the series which you are about to begin,
proceed to center attention on the word *COME*. This might
be done by saying, "A United Methodist bishop once said,
'If the gospel were to be put into one word, it would have

to be the word *COME.*' We are in full agreement with this statement. With this in mind we have selected as our text, Matthew 11:28: 'Come to me, all who labor and are heavy laden, and I will give you rest.' "

(2) The second method we call the CONTEXTUAL. Frequently it combines nicely with the textual approach. And well it may, for, as G. Campbell Morgan never tired of saying, "A text without its context is pretext." John R. W. Stott, expositor of our own day, gives support to this principle when he rightly accuses some ministers of preaching on texts outside their proper contexts *(The Preacher's Portrait,* p. 13). Indeed, whether a preacher uses the contextual approach in the actual shaping of an introduction or not, he exercises homiletical integrity only when he examines the whole literary unit of which his text is a part. Donald Bastian, a college pastor, insures this kind of integrity by outlining the material around his sermon Scripture, as well as around the text itself.

Contextual approaches abound. Three are listed here as typical: language, place, and custom. As a first step you have read and reread your Scripture lesson thoughtfully and prayerfully. Hopefully its origin, intent, and flavor are now yours.

In your initial consideration of the Scripture lesson you have noted the type of literature with which you are dealing— prophecy, poetry, legend, gospel, apocalypse, whatever. As you ponder the sermon passage in your mind a new and exciting pattern emerges—one you are eager to share with your people. A quick look in a homiletical commentary tells you that the rendering of the text in this pattern was intentional on the part of the translators. You learn that it is a valuable device to assist memory. The beginning of a helpful introduction thus emerges:

> A sk and you shall receive.
> S eek and you shall find.
> K nock and it shall be opened to you.
> A S K—is clearly one major thrust of the passage.

Here you have an example of the *linguistic* context which
can be presented within a frame of reference understandable
to laymen.

Next consider the context of *place*. Geography does make
a difference! Scientists have long known that culture is
formed in part by geographical position. Thus, in the warmer
climate of the Bible lands people move and think more slow-
ly; the siesta is universal; food must be carefully protected.

Let us suppose that you are preaching from the Acts of
the Apostles, and you note Paul's eagerness to preach the
gospel (chap. 19) : He "argued daily in the hall of Tyrannus."
You observe a footnote that says some ancient authorities
add the words, "from the fifth hour to the tenth," and a look
in a commentary tells you there is a good chance that the
reference to the time of day is authentic. You notice, too,
that these hours include the siesta period. By now you make
preliminary notes, eventually to flower in the introduction,
and perhaps in the outline of the sermon.

> Siesta time—hottest part of the day.
> People came to hear Paul anyway.
> Quite obviously he was a fascinating person.

In this case the geographical background—specifically the
consideration of climate and accompanying rest pattern—
has provided you with interesting introductory material.

Explore also the context of *custom*—the mores of the people. For example, suppose you are working on a sermon from
Luke 11, entitling it "The Friend at Midnight." Prayer is
your general theme, but for this specific sermon the urgency
of prayer has caught your imagination. Studying the passage,
you notice the curious clause, "My children are with me in
bed." In consulting a book on customs of Bible times you
learn that in Jesus' day houses were often of one room, with
a raised place in the center used for sleeping. The whole
family occupied this area. With this knowledge you have the
basis for genuinely interesting opening comments.

Always remember that the context is the background. Paint

it well and you will find yourself with the opportunity to paint in the foreground with clear perspective.

(3) Some sermons may well begin with the use of an appropriate ILLUSTRATION. The problem is to locate a story that fits your intent like a hand in a kid glove.

This approach is particularly appropriate and helpful when addressing a group unoriented to the subject at hand. For example, in case the audience is known to have only a smattering of Biblical knowledge, the specialized textual or contextual approaches will not do. Rather than allow interest to lag, attention may be captured by the use of a gripping narrative of general interest.

Observe these warnings, however. A story may be good in and of itself, but quite unrelated to the real frame of your theme. When a story is used in this way it is employed with a wrong motive. Illustration for illustration's sake is comparable to art for art's sake. An illustration may, of course, be enjoyed, but that should not be the purpose you have in mind. Your intent in using an illustration in your introduction should be to secure attention to the subject of your sermon.

Another warning is in order. Like much advertising, a good story can be a mere come-on, promising excellence but not producing it. The glitter turns out to be fool's gold, resulting in a disappointing letdown for both the audience and the preacher. In that case it defeats the very purpose for which it is intended.

(4) Another introductory technique is known as the LIFE-SITUATION method. In modern times, Harry Emerson Fosdick pioneered this method of attack. He took hold of a contemporary problem, spelled it out in vivid terms, and left people saying to themselves, "Why! I never knew preachers thought about things like that!" Our image of preachers has altered greatly since the 1920s and 30s—and 40s. Today we accept the life-situation method as valid and Biblical, and serving its purpose well.

Students of preaching would do well to read Fosdick's

article in the July 1928 issue of *Harpers*. That article turned
out to be a homiletical bombshell that changed many a man's
preaching.

Often this type of sermon begins with a life-situation question. So James S. Stewart opens his celebrated sermon, "The
Lord God Omnipotent Reigneth" with the question, "What
to you is the most important thing in all the world? What is
the thing without which you simply could not live?" He continues his introduction by offering options: home, job, health.
Then Professor Stewart gives the answer of John the Reve-
lator. The most important thing in all the world is the fact
that, "The Lord God omnipotent reigneth." Then follows
powerful preaching which fulfills every expectation aroused
by the introduction!

(5) Still another introductory approach is the making of
A SIMPLE AND DIRECT STATEMENT OF PURPOSE. This can be
brief, particularly if your people are already oriented to the
subject (as, for example, for a sermon in the midst of a
series). Like a modern jet, get into the air as soon as possible, using the runway only as long as necessary.

Precautions are in order here. Be sure your people do in
fact have the orientation you suppose. Will there be people
in attendance who were not there the previous Sunday or
two? If so, it will be necessary for you to review briefly, but
not boringly. Are the people truly prepared for this specific
truth? If not, what distinctive runway can you devise? This
requires careful judgment. Stay on the runway too long and
the people will lose interest and get restless. Get airborne
too soon and suffer the consequences of a forced landing.

The other point of caution refers to the way you state your
purpose. Presented in direct but attractive words, it can command attention; stated in flat and ordinary words it can prepare people for sleep.

(6) Still another type of beginning is the STRIKING STATE-
MENT OR QUOTATION. For a sermon "The Power of Belief,"
one could well start with Phillips Brooks's provocative statement: "There is nothing the unbeliever honors like belief."

Or in a sermon on "Christian Healing," you might, for example, commence with this statement, at once attention-getting and perfect preparation for the deeper truth you want to present: "Anger, indeed negative thoughts of any kind, poison both mind and body."

Caution yourself to fulfill what you have promised in such an opening statement. Do not allow your people to accuse you of clever (or not so clever!) deception by a perfectly marvelous opening sentence that leads nowhere.

Caution yourself, too, about the coloration of that opening statement. Moody once began his sermon by saying, "Go to hell; that is what I heard someone say as I walked into this auditorium tonight"; but that was Dwight Lyman Moody! If the personality of the speaker does not admit of radically startling statements, they will leave the poor man looking ridiculous. Or the people will get the impression, sometimes justified, that he is calling attention to himself by shocking them.

(7) Finally, there is the introduction for a SPECIAL OCCASION, such as a funeral. This is not the place for a striking opening statement of any kind. The atmosphere is somber, and the wise minister will minimize the dramatic. Already the family has suffered enough real-life drama! He may say simply: "We have assembled to pay tribute to our late and beloved friend, Robert White."

Or there may be the dedication of a church. In all probability the power of the occasion has produced the crowd; thus a grandiloquent story need not be given at all. In fact, it would be out of place. You may start right out by talking of God's house and its purposes.

George Buttrick mentions four characteristics of a good introduction: the raising of an issue, brevity, interest, and appropriateness. The latter, always applicable, is especially so for special-occasion preaching. Those opening words either harmonize or disharmonize with the atmosphere already present; thus, the minister must do some careful thinking about the event, capturing the mood and bending his introduction to the temper and atmosphere of the hour.

GENERAL HINTS ABOUT PRODUCING INTRODUCTIONS

(1) BE BRIEF. An introduction is the porch, not the house. Near Lexington, Kentucky, is a Civil War house whose fascination is its oddity. The man who built the home ran out of money before he could complete it. The result is a magnificent white, four-columned frontage without the anterior and major part of the house. When taking the side country road the full perspective looms into view, and the distinct impression is left that the man built little more than a porch. Some sermons are like that! It is a homiletical crime for a preacher to get to 11:50 on Sunday morning and announce— "That, by way of introduction."

The introduction should only be long enough to accomplish its implied purpose—to introduce the subject—and no longer. The length, of course, will vary according to the subject, the level of understanding of the audience, and the occasion. But the rambling introduction should be carefully avoided. Said Spurgeon to his students of preaching: "Gentlemen, don't go creeping into your subject as some swimmers go into the water: first to the ankles, and then to the knees, and then to the waist, and then to the shoulders: plunge in at once over head and ears." This is good advice and many have heeded it to bring blessings to themselves and God's people. An old woman said of the Welsh preacher, John Owen, that he was so long spreading the table she lost her appetite for the meal.

(2) TAKE TIME. Paterson Smyth, British trainer of preachers, had it right when he said, "You can make them listen, if you pay the price." The price which must be paid is time and hard work.

W. E. Sangster was one who paid the price. His third rule for making introductions was: Be arresting. Be brief, and be interesting were his first two rules, and they take time too.

But to be arresting is the prior goal. The preparation of an arresting introduction may take time—but it will be time well spent.

(3) A third hint merits careful observation: USE A VARIETY OF APPROACHES. Seven of many possible techniques were outlined in this chapter; you yourself can create other ways of setting out on a sermonic venture. This is well. "Never do the same thing always" is a sound homiletical law. To follow it keeps the preacher's mind sharp and the people alert. And there is a valuable side benefit—you will not have the teens snickering at you for always doing things "the same old way."

(4) The fourth suggestion is really more than a hint. It reminds us of a basic truth about the relation of form and content. Homiletics deals most especially with form, and by that very fact can lure the unsuspecting into the trap of believing cleverly wrought work constitutes the essence and end of all preaching. HOMILETICS, INCLUDING SKILLS FOR PRODUCING INTRODUCTIONS, IS ACTUALLY THE SERVANT OF ETERNAL TRUTH, NEVER AN END IN ITSELF! It is the burning truth of the gospel which turns people to God and His salvation at all levels. It is actually possible for sermons to be so nice, so homiletically perfect, that the attention of the people becomes focused more on the craftsmanship of the sermon than on Christ.

A QUESTION THAT COULD BE SIGNIFICANT

When should the introduction be written? Andrew W. Blackwood counts himself among those who prefer to compose the introduction after the sermon is written. After all, goes the argument, do not authors write their prefaces last? Others, like Ilion T. Jones, exhort us to put together beginning statements at the outset of the writing enterprise. After all, shouldn't one reduce the introduction to writing in its proper place? Why not write from start to finish uninterrupted.

Ralph L. Lewis comes closer to the Blackwood school when he lists the steps in the construction of a sermon in this sequence:

1. Formulate the purpose.
2. Select the chief supporting points.
3. Properly label chief supporting points.
4. Select materials to develop the supporting points.
5. Plan the introduction.
6. Plan the conclusion.

Experiment for yourself. At what point is writing the introduction most feasible for you? You may well discover that it varies from sermon to sermon. One time the perfect introduction comes right off; at another time the conclusion breaks its way into your consciousness; at still another time the outline falls into shape first thing. The important matter is that it be executed when seasoned.

V. THE SHAPING OF THE BODY

The Yale Lectures on Preaching say many things about structure. Different structure types are quite acceptable, but there is one fundamental principle on which there is complete agreement: *There must be structure.*

Listeners, especially the untrained, may not be conscious of the presence of structure. But all will recognize the presence or absence of *point.* And that is the purpose of structure. Point is the effect or the product of structure.

Stephen Leacock's famous man who got on his horse and rode off in all directions is very like the celebrated and pathetic preacher who "took a text and went everywhere preaching the gospel."

Meaning is the product of order, and that is why the ancient proverb, "Order is heaven's first law," carries immediate and built-in authority. We know instinctively that the proverb puts into focus a fundamental and significant truth. Paul himself recognized this truth when he wrote that "all things should be done decently and in order" (I Cor. 14:40).

Order looms large as a dimension of good preaching. See the genius of John Wesley's classic three points on the use of money:

> Gain all you can
> Save all you can
> Give all you can

Ordered points provide at least three great benefits: (1) A map for the speaker. How can one get lost with a map before him? (2) A guide to the listener. How can people get lost if their guide leads the way? (3) A sense of march to

the sermon. How can the goal be missed if points move pur-
posively?

STEPS TO BODY BUILDING

(1) STEP ONE: FORMULATE YOUR PURPOSE. John Henry
Jowett gives us guidance in this classic statement: "I am of
the conviction that no sermon is ready for preaching, nor
ready for writing out, until we can express its theme in a
short, pregnant sentence as clear as a crystal. I find the getting of that sentence the hardest, the most exacting, and the
most fruitful labor in my study. To compel oneself to fashion
that sentence, to dismiss every word that is vague, ragged,
ambiguous, to think oneself through to a form of words which
defines the theme with scrupulous exactness—this is surely
one of the most vital and essential factors in the making of
a sermon: and I do not think any sermon ought to be preached
or even written, until that sentence has emerged, clear and
lucid as a cloudless moon" *(The Preacher, His Life and
Work,* p. 133).

Notice the words "hardest," "exacting," "fruitful." Notice again the final phrase, "clear and lucid as a cloudless
moon."

*Put the single sentence or purpose at the top of each ser-
mon and do it religiously.* An example of such a sentence is:
The purpose of this sermon is to make clear the meaning of
the new birth.

Now, in working out that statement you have both general and specific goals to determine. At the general level,
you must ask: Is the purpose of this sermon to teach? to inspire? to evangelize? to edify? What is the purpose? Nail
down your answer. At the specific level, you must ask: If
this is a teaching sermon, what particular truth am I to spell
out? If to inspire, to what purpose? If to evangelize, how can
I bring people to the actual point of decision? If to edify,
what nutrients do my people need just now?

These preliminary but altogether crucial questions you will

ask first, and then go on to reduce to writing your purpose, in line with the text and theme God's Spirit has assigned.

(2) STEP TWO: PHRASE YOUR TOPIC. At some early point the topic must be given verbal shape, especially because it helps you isolate your theme—but also because of the scheduling demands of the local newspaper and the church office which is responsible for the printed or duplicated order of worship. Wednesday before noon is a reasonable deadline.

Time was when a good deal was said in the homiletical literature and classroom lectures on what Madison Avenue could teach the preacher about constructing his sermon topics. Every effort was to be put forth to make sermon topics not only appealing, but striking and sensational, too. After all, surely a smartly dressed topic will bring people to church! That reasoning sounds good, but the facts have not borne out its validity. Thousands of pastors have produced well-turned and exciting topics, but all to little avail. Probably this was in part due to the fact that sensationalism possesses no magic.

Do people really want sermons on topics like these? "A Shave in the Devil's Barber Shop," or "Seven Ducks in a Muddy Pond" (Naaman!). People may laugh at this kind of topic making and preaching and think it cute, but it soon grows stale and becomes ludicrous. Also there quickly emerges in the mind of the thoughtful minister the question of the ethics of leading people only to the fringes of the gospel, if indeed to that! And his people will get no farther unless he leads them into the fertile pasture of the Word.

A sound homiletical rule is this: *Sensationalism neither brings people to, nor nurtures them in, the eternal gospel.* The vehicle for performing that twin miracle is the sober (but not painful!) preaching of the Word of God.

But we can learn from Madison Avenue by way of calm consideration. Modern advertising science has taught us the advantage of using few words. Three words communicate best; four or five do well; beyond that the effectiveness diminishes. People passing by the church bulletin board in busy traffic will be lucky to see three words! The point is, avoid unnecessary words.

Madison Avenue has also taught us the importance of projecting ideas in word pictures. In advertising, a dog, a child, or a pretty girl are sure winners. It would be pretty hard to get these into the minister's topic, but the picture principle is clear. "Care in All Things" pictures nothing; "Spread Your Money Wisely" conjures an image immediately.

Throughout all this it is important to remember two things: (1) the topic must be true to the text, and (2) the topic must describe faithfully the actual sermon thrust. If possible let three or four words right out of your Scripture passage become your topic. "Be Strong, Fear Not!" is perfect for a sermon on Isaiah 35:3-4. "God's Straight Paths" is both solid and adequate for Proverbs 3:5-6.

(3) STEP THREE: CHOOSE YOUR POINTS. You are to speak on the Holy Spirit; your purpose is down in black and white; the passage is before you. Your next task is to isolate points— not to put them in final phrasing just now, only to select them. As the theme turns in your mind, the skeleton begins to emerge: cleansing—that is one work of the Spirit; peace— that is a product of His coming; capacity to serve—that too is the fruitage of His work. Cleansing, peace, service—yes, those are authentic. There. You have made your decision.

Like topics, points must be true to the text and in line with the sermon's fixed purpose. All parts of the sermon must work together toward a common end. Sorting out your points may take a while. Do not rush the process; let them "come."

(4) STEP FOUR: DETERMINE THE NOMENCLATURE OF YOUR POINTS. You now have three points—cleansing, peace, service—but at this juncture they are only in rough form. Perfected terminology has not yet developed. The mulling process continues and as it does, there occurs to you the possibility of couching the three points alliteratively. You decide that if you could find three suitable words, beginning with the same letter of the alphabet, it might accomplish two

things: (1) it could simplify communication and (2) alliteration could assist the memory. You can try the letter P: you already have Peace. *Cleansing* suggests *Purity.* As you try to think of a third P to express service there comes to your mind the New Testament word, *Power.* And so an outline has emerged:

I. Peace
II. Purity
III. Power

The order of these three points is logical and proper. Everyone is looking for peace, inner peace, so you have a strong kick-off point. Purity, closely related to power, must precede it if power is to be godly and God-pleasing. Power makes the perfect climax for a sermon on the work of the Holy Spirit.

Do not become obsessed with the idea that you must always use alliteration. You can make yourself look ridiculous if you do so. And it may force you to use less exact and specific words. But alliteration can be effective if used occasionally and well.

(5) STEP FIVE: SELECT YOUR SUPPORTING MATERIALS. Right through this whole process you have been gathering materials: arguments, examples, word pictures of all kinds. You are now ready to select from the mass of material just what suits the purpose of your text. If, by this time, you still find yourself without sufficient material, you will go to other resources—books, files, etc.—and sift and sort until you are in possession of enough to make a full and well-rounded sermon.

You are preparing to do final placing of matter, putting illustrations and data under each head. Some preliminary placing comes quickly and naturally, but your task just now is simply selecting: this is good, that will fit, here is an apropos illustration.

(6) STEP SIX: ARRANGE THE WHOLE INTO AN OUTLINE. Says Harold Ockenga, "I spend the most time on my outline,

so that it is logical, alliterative, parallelistic, and easy to remember" (*How to Prepare and Deliver Better Sermons*, pp. 51-52). This is good counsel.

The first secret of a good outline is this: *classify points consistently.* Take an illustration outside the preaching field. For example, you are to address the local horticultural club on flowers. You may classify points under heads like roses, sweet peas, and hydrangeas; these headings are consistent. You may not discuss roses, sweet peas, and annuals; these headings are not parallel. Again, you may give a talk on annuals and perennials, but not on annuals and roses. Keep categories consistent.

A second secret: *maintain parallelism.* The great poet and philosopher of India, Rabindranath Tagore, said of Jesus' words, "Except ye be converted, and become as little children, ye shall not enter into the kingdom of heaven"—these words, said Tagore, are the most beautiful in Scripture. Commenting on this, E. Stanley Jones gives us a perfect outline: "The three stand together—(1) 'be converted'—a new direction; (2) 'become as little children'—a new spirit; (3) 'enter the kingdom of God'—a new sphere of living. The three give the essence of conversion" (*Conversion*, p. 40). Observe how Dr. Jones achieves this telling parallelism: First, by the imperative mood: be, become, enter; next by repetition, the repetition of the meaningful adjective "new." Direction, spirit, and living become new.

The preacher skilled in the employment of parallelism knows the value and impact of surprise changes. Someone prayed, "Fill us all with that power of love that believes all things, hopes all things, and never gives up." Note that the twins "love believes all things" and "love hopes all things" are given an injection of energy by a quite different kind of statement, a contrasting statement: "Love never gives up." The parallelism of thought is actually strengthened by the change of pace.

The great James S. Stewart's skill at parallel outlining surfaces in a sermon like "The Gospel of the Ascension," based on Luke 24:51-53, John 16:17, and Ephesians 4:8:

I. It was expedient for the spiritualizing of religion
II. It was expedient for the universalizing of the gospel
III. It was expedient for the energizing of evangelism
IV. It was expedient for the fortifying of faith

The genius of the outline is manifold: the formula welds the sermon together; language is carefully chosen—*expedient* is a strong word; alliteration assists both preacher and people in remembering; *ing* words describe accurately; final nouns—religion, gospel, evangelism, faith—supply defiinite New Testament content.

A third secret of effective outline construction: *build to a climax.* There is progress in every good sermon; it moves perceptibly and definitely toward a clear and worthy goal. This should be evident in the outline.

To do this a variety of techniques come to our aid. For one, do not give away too much in your opening point; otherwise, the unfolding of your idea, like the premature flowering of a blossom, loses its element of surprise. Attention is dissipated. You may or may not wish to reveal the whole three- or four-step outline at the outset of your sermon. When you do so it is for the purpose of heightening anticipation. Its purpose is to give a preview of good things to come.

The first point, the kick-off point, holds a highly important position. But it over-plays its role if it encroaches on the points that follow. The sense of progress toward the goal is achieved in part by a proper reserve and a proper sequence.

Middle points continue the feel of ascendency, the sense that the listener is climbing a ladder.

The final point prepares for the emotional climax in the conclusion. Indeed, it leads to the very gates of the finale. Notice the ladder effect, with the feel of climax at the end, in the Shaker credo:

1. Dignity in Work
2. Serenity in Spirit
3. Excellence in Everything

The fact that each category is larger than the preceding provides the march toward climax, and helps account for the magic of this simple outline.

Give attention to the *psychological sequence of points.* In pro and con argument, put the pros before the cons. This is psychologically sound in that it helps avoid undue negative feelings toward the message. Get your audience depressed, antagonistic, or deafened, and you have lost them. In the handling of negative material always remember the nature of faith—it is a construct, not a "destruct." When negatives, of necessity, need giving out, rush in positives to take their place. But whenever truth can be positively rather than negatively stated in the first place, choose the first alternative. The essential task of the preacher is affirmation. Notice that all save one of the tenets of the isolated KERYGMA are positive, and the negative one (the cross) is made positive by the resurrection.

Learn to *catch the feel of points in sequence.* Demosthenes commented, "Persuasion is as dependent upon the order of the arguments as upon the arguments themselves." Horace, discussing poetry, observed that, "The beauty of order consists in saying just now what just now ought to be said, and postponing for the present all the rest." Placement of material with a view to audience palpability is high on the homiletician's priority list.

The sixth secret is *unity,* immediately observable as an underlying assumption of the above five "secrets." Simple enough in principle, it is difficult to put into practice. A few suggestions are in order.

Keep to one subject. You are discussing *one* truth, not the universe. Donald Bastian's tripartite rule for preaching is pertinent: (1) Say one thing; (2) Say one thing concretely; (3) Say one thing relevantly.

When asked how to make a speech, Winston Churchill answered in a style true to his form. Said he to his questioner, "Get one idea; one, not two. Give it a whack! Talk on a little while, then give your idea another whack! Talk some more; give it still another whack! Proceed like this until you come to the finale, and give it a terrific whack!"

The model of single-theme-unity is the tree, not the brushpile. The tree has a trunk, branches, and leaves. It has order. To be sure, it has variety, but variety in order. The trunk is the main stream of thought, the branches its points, the leaves its illustrations and quotations. The brushpile too frequently typifies the sermon of the inept, careless, or lazy preacher. It is an error to suppose that a lot of words, even with fairly good illustrations here and there, will translate a brushpile into a tree. Glittering stories, a nice voice, and a confident manner may work in concert to hide the lack of unity for a time. But the problem with this clever trick is at least twofold: (1) you can fool some of the people some of the time, but not all the people all the time, and (2) you will fail to develop in your people the fundamental unity of the Christian faith. Both are serious, the latter the more serious. It will leave your people wide open to cultic movements which *can* and will provide them systematic models. God's Word, properly presented and projected, provides the toolage and ground for handling both major and minor problems in faith and life.

One pathway to unity is *limiting the number of points.* F. W. Robertson of Brighton, England, developed what might be termed a two-pole homiletic. He would find a pair of points for interpreting a passage. Sometimes executed dialogically, he would pit opposites against one another, coming out at the end with the balanced truth that was his sermonic goal. In any event, the juggling of a pair of points through the sermon was his technique, his method of grappling with a single Biblical point of faith.

Alexander Maclaren had three or four points. Augustine and others have argued for three as the perfect number. It is true that there is a kind of magic about the number three: completeness (like the uneven seven). Three, somehow, is suggestive of not too few nor too many. There seems to be a sense of just-rightness about three. Attention is held easier

with three than more. But you should allow yourself no hint
of superstition about the number; when two, four, or five
points are required to do the job, do not hesitate! The point
is economy in the service of effective communication.

Rarely should a preacher use more than five points. In
fact, the man who can sustain attention with even five points
proves his unusual ability. When disunity emerges, attention
fades. The unusual man maintains the sense of unity throughout, even with many points; such was W. E. Sangster when
he preached his celebrated ten-point sermon on what revival
would do (see *Dr. Sangster,* p. 173).

The same law applies to subpoints. Dividing outlines into
points under points under points may be suited to classroom
use, but is ill suited to public address. About as complex as
one can get—and this only if the content and outline are
good—is an analysis comparable to this one on the topic,
"Maintaining the Spiritual Glow":

    I. The nature of the spiritual glow
      A. One must have a governing appetite for God
      B. One must have a growing awareness of God
      C. One must have a gripping ambition toward God
    II. The nurture of the spiritual glow
      A. The mind must be informed
      B. The emotions must be involved
      C. The will must be inspired

Cicero's principle of "careful negligence" constitutes wise
advice to the man who is tempted to use too many major and
subpoints. Select only your best ideas, and, by an act of the
will if necessary, carefully neglect all the rest.

Unity is also assisted by repetition. This should not be
done crudely nor to the point of becoming boring—a common pitfall for preachers—but with the telling finesse of the
ringing motif of a Beethoven symphony. Bill Stidger, long-
time preacher and teacher of homiletics, discussed the "sym-
phonic sermon." Designed to inspire and invigorate by the
repeated rhythms of a great idea, the truth fixed itself in-

delibly in the listener's mind. A great symphony is marked
by the repetition of a grand musical idea; secondary musical
ideas act as continuity and supporting material. This is the
skilled repeating of columns in a cathedral, arches in a
cloister, lined trees along a Champs Elyses.

PUTTING IT ALL TOGETHER

With the preceding suggestions in mind the preacher remains faced with the task of constructing his sermon. He can
learn much from those who are known to be masters of the
homiletical art. The budding pianist learns as he watches the
technique and listens to the magic of a Rubinstein; an under-
study painter watches a seasoned Italian artist copy the
masterworks in the Vatican; the medical student exposes himself to the deft movement of the hands of the skilled surgeon.

Four men, discussed in other connections elsewhere in this
volume, here serve as models: Paul S. Rees, C. Ralston Smith,
Richard C. Halverson, and Harold J. Ockenga.

(1) PAUL S. REES. Prayerfully, and with the needs of his
audience in mind, Dr. Rees goes through his "jewel box"
(3 x 5 cards with prospective sermon subjects, topics, texts,
outlines, illustrations, bibliographies), and makes his theme
selection. That determined, he makes a fresh study of the
chosen text within its context. At this point he assigns himself the reading of the passage over and again, using several
versions, until the natural and intended meaning emerges
loud and clear. His use of translations to assist him is worth
underscoring and the appendix to this chapter carries a partial
listing of English translations of the Scriptures.

Getting a clear picture of the text-in-its-context may require the reading of an entire book of the Bible. This exposure is essential to adequate Biblical preaching. So is the
examination of exegetical sources, Rees's next step. This requires the study of such a work as *The Expositor's Greek
New Testament*.

Following that, Paul Rees discovers how other preachers

have treated the text. However, he states that he finds few sermons helpful; those most helpful are mostly expository.

All the while notes are being made under selected headings, and quotations and illustrations are being gathered. Only those pictures which illumine his points with high-level precision are employed; illustrations that do not really fit are refused.

Now he is ready to type a set of notes, the shape of his material being formed sufficiently to take this step. The final procedure is the typing of a complete manuscript.

(2) C. RALSTON SMITH follows a sermon building program which is somewhat different and considerably simpler. He begins with sheets of paper on which he makes notations. Notes accumulate through the week as he reads and thinks. When materials are sufficiently far along, he arranges them in orderly sequence. During all this time, he constantly reviews, mulling it all over in his mind so that by Sunday he will have his idea firmly fixed.

As pastor of a busy church he does not write his sermons out in full. He gives his reasons: "With two messages each Sunday—one for duplicate morning services, one for vespers —and a church school lesson for adults (a book-of-the-Bible study), I have neither time nor inclination to do this" (*How to Prepare and Deliver Better Sermons*, p. 10).

His custom is to go over the full outline at home on Sunday morning. Upon arrival at church he reduces the outline to a few statements under major heads, paying particular attention to quotations, illustrations, and poetry.

(3) RICHARD C. HALVERSON makes a serious effort to begin his sermon preparation on Monday, and sometimes he gets ahead by a week or two. By reading the Scripture source through as often as necessary, he achieves a sense of "its general intent." Usually, after a number of readings, the passage outlines itself and the topic crystalizes. He refuses to use sensational topics "designed principally to get attention." "Most of my topics are lifted verbatim from the Scripture,"

he says, and he makes sure that the true theme of his message is compressed into the topic.

His discipline includes putting the sermon into a topical sentence; college courses in journalism helped him to learn this important skill. It is difficult to master this skill but a man like John Henry Jowett considered it one of the most important techniques a preacher can learn. (See Steps to Body Building, [1] of this present chapter.)

Dr. Halverson does a verse-by-verse analysis, using legal-sized lined paper. He writes verse numbers in the margin, copies each verse after its number, and records his own commentary beneath every verse. He finds assistance in this exercise by reference to such works as Robertson Nicoll's *The Expositor's Greek New Testament,* Vincent's *Word Studies,* and A. T. Robertson's *Word Pictures.* Young's *Concordance* helps him too, because there the original Biblical words are provided along with references.

Notes are finally recorded on four to seven 5½ x 8½ sheets, and put into final form Saturday afternoon or evening —sometimes even early Sunday morning. "I am most proficient in their use," says he of these note sheets, "when they are as fresh as possible." The introduction and conclusion have previously been typed in full; also typed completely are sensitive passages and key sentences. He gives special attention to word choice—Roget's *Thesaurus* helps—and constantly tries to improve expression. He was taught to "abhor mediocrity."

(4) HAROLD J. OCKENGA, President of Gordon-Conwell Seminary, was formerly pastor of historic Park Street Congregational Church, Boston. In preparation for a series of expository sermons—he usually preaches expository sermons —he reads and rereads the book of the Bible from which he is to preach. The bulk of his time is invested in formulating the outline so that the thoughts on the passage fall into memorable and meaningful sequence.

All significant thoughts he has on the subject at hand are

listed. Consulting critical commentaries, he does his best to insure correct interpretation.

His next step is to pull supporting information and illustration from the file and book index. Sometimes he consults practical commentaries for still more assistance.

The final act for Dr. Ockenga is the dictation of the message. He states that his purpose is: "to be able to express myself carefully and well."

Modern Versions

John Wesley, *Explanatory Notes on the New Testament* (1755).

The Revised Version (1881 and 1885).

The Twentieth Century New Testament (1898-1901, 1904, Moody reprint 1961).

Arthur S. Way, *The Letters of St. Paul to Seven Churches and Three Friends,* second edition (1906).

Richard F. Weymouth, *The New Testament in Modern Speech* (1903).

James Moffatt, *A New Translation of the Bible* (N.T. 1913; O.T. 1924; together 1926; final revision 1935 by Harper).

The Holy Scriptures According to the Massoretic Text, A New Translation (1923).

Helen B. Montgomery, *The Centenary Translation of the New Testament,* 2 vol. (1924).

Smith-Goodspeed, *The Bible: An American Translation* (1931). (Note T. J. Meek's revision by University of Chicago Press, *The Complete Bible, An American Translation,* 1939.)

Charles B. Williams, *The New Testament in the Language of the People* (1937).

Confraternity Edition (N.T. 1941; O.T. 1948; note recent parallel R.S.V.).

The Bible in Basic English (N.T. 1941; O.T. 1949).

J. W. C. Wand, *The New Testament Letters* (1943; a few corrections in the edition of 1946).

Ronald A. Knox, *The New Testament of Our Lord and Savior Jesus Christ* (1944; *Old Testament with Apocrypha,* in two volumes 1948, 59).

Berkeley Version (N.T. 1945; O.T. 1959).

Charles Kingsley Williams, *The New Testament, A New Translation in Plain English* (1952).

Revised Standard Version (1952).

E. V. Rieu, *The Four Gospels* (1952); note to The Acts of the Apostles by his son, C. H. Rieu (1957).

Kenneth S. Wuest, *The Gospels* (1956); *Acts through Ephesians* (1958); *Philippians through Revelation* (1960).

Amplified (N.T. 1958; O.T. 1962).

J. B. Phillips, *New Testament in Modern English* (1958).

New English Bible (N.T. 1961).

Olaf M. Norlie, *Simplified New Testament* (1961) (Same as *Children's Simplified New Testament*).

Joseph Gelineau, *The Psalms, A New Translation* (Fontana Books, 1963).

The American Standard Version (1901; New American Standard Bible, N.T. 1963).

William F. Beck, *The New Testament in the Language of Today* (1964).

F. F. Bruce, *The Letters of Paul, An Expanded Paraphrase Printed in Parallel with the Revised Version* (1965).

Good News for Modern Man (1966).

Kenneth N. Taylor, *The Living Bible* (1971).

The New Scofield Reference Bible (Z. S. English, 1967).

Clarence Jordan, *The Cotton Patch Version of Paul's Epistles* (1963).

VI. THE MAKING OF CONCLUSIONS

"My sermons are not to be remembered," announced W. E. Sangster, "but translated." For a sermon actually to get translated, the conclusion must drive home the central substance of the message.

WAYS TO DO IT

(1) Sometimes SUMMARIZE. Here is your sermon in a nutshell. You recap to nail down a specific truth. Your points should not be rehearsed in classroom fashion; that turns people off. But they should be reiterated in fresh language, with both emotional and intellectual appeal. Such a summary has power to turn people very much on.

This technique is especially useful in a teaching sermon. Suppose you have attempted to show that knowledge and self-control, time-honored virtues, are significant, but that self-giving is superior and, in the Christian faith, makes knowledge and self-control possible and truly meaningful. The makings of the fresh summary language for such a theme might be this:

> Socrates said, "Know thyself."
> Cicero said, "Control thyself."
> But Jesus said, "Give thyself."

(2) Often TELL HOW. Paul S. Rees makes clear that there are preaching opportunities in which "it would be unforgivable not to show 'wherein' and not to deal with 'how to.'" He refers to the conclusion demanding concrete application. "Give the steps," Dr. Rees continues. "Reduce the general

to the specific. Name the action (or actions) that should be taken, beginning now. Press the point in lovingly relentless thrust to the will" (*How To Prepare And Deliver Better Sermons,* p. 38).

The "how to" conclusion demands perhaps our greatest thought and effort, precisely because it is so difficult to tell how in specific and concrete ways. Much exhortation from the pulpit is weak, more like the pussyfoot creep than the tiger's sure stride. Frequently exhortation is louder than it is clear. (We would do well to remember Sam Johnson's classic line of criticism: "Sir, you raise your voice when you should reinforce your argument.")

Come to grips with what must be done by Christians of strong convictions:

- Write a letter of protest to your local TV channel. Sex and violence must go. The address is in the morning bulletin.

- Has misunderstanding resulted in an interpersonal breakdown at work? Don't argue and talk back. That is the beginning of a fruitless war. Invite the boss home to dinner!

- Are you fed up with the pornographic literature at the corner store? If so, you can do something about it. The PTA of one American town organized a boycott of their local supermarket, thus effecting quick clean-up of the magazine rack.

(3) Occasionally SHOW ANGER. You have a perfect right to display anger and to anger your people in the spirit of Jesus casting the money changers out of the temple. The mothers in the community PTA drama cited just above moved angrily. Someone had stirred them. Was it a minister?

One minister became thoroughly angered at horse betting. He watched it rob men of their money and in turn rob families of bread. Observing personality disintegration on the one hand, and the burgeoning coffers of the race track managers on the other, the angry preacher went to the track himself, collected a fistful of discarded betting stubs, and carried them into his pulpit the next Sunday morning. With fire in his eye he concluded his sermon with the following words: "These symbolize money used for downright wicked purposes. My business today," he said, holding the stubs for all to see, "is to expose the wretchedness of it all! Are you with me? Then let's do something about it."

The man whose mother suffered the loss of her life at the hands of a drunken driver, is not very happy about the liquor industry. The wife whose husband died of lung cancer possesses a vivid awareness of the tobacco trap. These are occasions for sermons which may fittingly be concluded in anger.

But one warning is in order. Save the angry conclusions for reasons worth anger. Jesus did not express anger in every sermon!

(4) Frequently ILLUSTRATE. One of the best ways to wind up a sermon is with a gripping illustration (unless, of course, you have used your full complement of illustrations in the body). This is especially effective when the sermon's argument has been continuous and somewhat exacting. In that case the conclusion is no place for still another argument, even in different words. But the illustration chosen must argue. It must convince, and in order to persuade, it must be crystal clear and perfectly apt.

Actually, many sermons can be "made" by a story which has the capacity to focus attention powerfully on the theme at hand. One would do well to keep a file of illustrations with just such an aim in mind. For example, Father Damien proved his dedication to the mission leper colony by his own contraction of the dreaded disease; Rudyard Kipling's Gungadene and Shakespeare's murder scene from Macbeth—all such are potentially and homiletically useful in the setting of a sermon conclusion. Adapted they must be; that is assumed. Used wisely, prayerfully, and meaningfully, an illus-

tration can clinch the message you hope to drive home to
God's people.

(5) Always IDENTIFY with your audience. Then your people will get the message. But if you keep yourself at arms'
length, even subtly, you communicate to them either lack of
genuine concern or superiority. Even in the matter of repen-
tance, you must identify with the unconverted man. You must
feel for him. You must see and feel yourself in his place.
After all, you yourself once lacked commitment. And if the
"forgive us our trespasses" part of the Lord's Prayer is to be
prayed sincerely, the minister will pray for fresh cleansing
for himself as well as for his people.

Perhaps your best opportunity for identification makes itself known in the hurts of your listeners. People do know
pretty much from the start of a sermon whether or not the
preacher identifies with the suffering they know; but in the
conclusion their awareness can be greatly sharpened. Often
their sense of your identification resides in the feeling tone
you project in the conclusion more than in what you actually
verbalize. Your actual attitude—understanding of their situation, openness to any workable solution, knowledge at deeper
levels, quiet modesty about coming to answers, sensitivity
to the real struggle of life—that magic, but authentic, mood
is sensed by churchgoers.

A concerned preacher makes a concerned people. And conclusions are "naturals" for showing concern.

SOME THINGS TO AVOID

(1) MORALIZING. A quick way to insult your hearers is
to tack onto every sermon an Aesop's Fable ending: "The
moral is. . . ." Give people credit: they can figure some things
for themselves. A well-known preacher tells of the woman
parishioner who said, "Pastor, I like your sermons but my
intelligence is insulted when you draw the obvious moral."
This is not to say that you should never conclude by pointing
out the lesson God intended in the passage of Scripture which

was expounded in your sermon. But it is for you to gauge the intellectual level of your audience; say only enough to communicate the truth at hand. It may well be that if your message has been clearly stated you can leave it to the Spirit of God and the human spirit to make applications as individually needed.

(2) STOPPING AFTER YOU ARE THROUGH is perhaps the worst of the sins in making conclusions. George Chadwick, American composer, instructed his students, "Never finish a thing after it is done." William Jennings Bryan's mother leveled with him after an evening's address with these poignant words: "Will, you missed several good opportunities to sit down."

Some sermons just "ravel out at the end." Like old soldiers, they die without notice, just fading away. But they need not and should not! They must be succinct rather than rambling, climactic rather than flat.

Albert W. Palmer used to say to his preaching classes: "Conclude your sermons like a player piano. The old player pianos," he commented, "went lickety bang, then all of a sudden stopped. Just like that! The piece finished, the music quit! And that is the way to stop a sermon."

(3) STOPPING BEFORE YOU ARE THROUGH is a danger, too. It is not as risky as stopping after finishing! But it is a danger nonetheless.

At all costs, wrap your sermon up completely. Make sure you have tucked in all the loose ends. But then stop! Abrupt conclusions are rarer but far more effective than overlong ones.

(4) INTRODUCING NEW MATERIAL constitutes a serious threat to successful conclusions. In debating, no new material is permitted in final speeches. That is a good rule! To bring in fresh data at that point of the dialog is unfair. And in a sermon it is unfair, too. Hopefully, lively dialog between you and your hearers has taken place as you delivered your sermon. Fresh material at the end will only serve to confuse that dialog instead of bringing out of it a clear conclusion.

(5) GENERALIZING is a ground for valid criticism of many sermon conclusions. *Specificity* yields high-level homiletical returns. It should be the preacher's goal to send hearers away from each service knowing quite fully the exact point of the sermon. People return to hear a preacher who leaves them with worthwhile truth specifically and insightfully announced.

And let's face temptation squarely. Fuzziness results from laziness; crystal clarity is the fruit of careful craftsmanship. Easy street produces nothing in particular; hard work and earnest prayer yield something in particular. You must make your choice.

(6) SCOLDING. It hardly seems necessary to say that scolding drives people away. Nonsupportive, abrasive statements, in a society oriented to a supportive psychology, are not only ineffectual but positively injurious. For the preacher it means the eventual loss of the backing of his people. The pastor who scolded his gathered church for not attending, had not stopped to realize that the offenders were not there to hear his admonitions. And when the absentees hear about their pastor's scoldings indirectly by word of mouth, they are all the more turned away from the church. A scolding preacher only reveals his own frustration. He presents a perfect example of what the psychologist calls projection.

There is, of course, definite place for the prophet's "no." The minister may be required at God's command to direct a negative word to his people. But careful study reveals that Jesus always spoke in the context of love. He was ever motivated and moved by the best interests of his people.

Clovis G. Chappell has summed up the principle at hand deftly and in vivid picture: "No man has a right so to preach as to send his hearers away on flat tires. Every discouraging sermon is a wicked sermon. . . . A discouraged man is not an asset but a liability."

(7) ANNOUNCING THE CONCLUSION is unnecessary. Just conclude. To announce the conclusion is to divert attention. The teens fidget, the adults breathe a polite and inner sigh

of relief. The preacher has succeeded perfectly in focusing their attention on getting out of church.

It is better to surprise your people; conclude before they scarcely know what has happened. End like the player piano. They will like you for it. But more important, the message will be uppermost in their minds.

(8) REPEATING TOO OFTEN THE SAME TYPES OF CONCLUSIONS. The law of variety applies here as it does elsewhere. Often evangelistically minded speakers bring their sermons to a close with an appeal for decision, couched almost always in the same kind of language. We may well leave that pattern to the Billy Grahams and the professional evangelists whose peculiar gifts bring people to decision.

Some preachers find themselves repeatedly using an illustration. This *is* an excellent way to conclude, as indicated earlier, provided the story feelingly focuses attention on the truth you desire to emphasize. But even if developed skills would permit you to "pull it off" every time, wisdom dictates enacting the discipline of variety. A little imagination will supply listeners with spice, surprise, and suspense, and yourself with the reward of creative accomplishment.

YOU WILL DO WELL TO REMEMBER

(1) END GRANDLY AND CLIMACTICALLY. This does not mean oratorically! But end the sermon at the point of climax —the high, noble, and solemn point. Anticlimax robs the conclusion of impact. In a sermon on "The Hope of the Gospel," why not end this way:

> It's true. Actually true! We are sons and daughters of the resurrection.

Or for a message on "God in Human Suffering," words like these from James Stewart's book of sermons, *The Strong Name:*

> ". . . be sure of this—no sorrow will have been wasted, if you come through it with a little more of the light of the

Lord visible in your face and shining in your soul " ("God
and the Fact of Suffering," p. 155).

These are climactic words indeed.

(2) END GENUINELY. After all, at this point you share
your deepest convictions. Any trace of artificiality vitiates
the strength of those convictions.

Suppose you preach on some such topic as "The Christian
Up Against It," the theme being hope and disillusionment.
A spineless conclusion might be:

> We all know the world is bad, very bad. But somehow God
> will see us through.

Needed is a sure word of hope and redemption like this:

> The very disillusionment of today is the raw material of the
> Christian hope.

Let the mighty excitements of the eternal gospel touch people
to their inner being. That is done not by any trick of oratory,
but by sharing your profoundest beliefs, tested and found
sure in the crucible of life.

Structurally the conclusion must not be a mere addendum;
that militates against genuineness. Endings must be natural,
organically related to the whole sermon. Canned, tacked-on
conclusions out of a book can hardly be sure vehicles of
authenticity even though perfect in form.

(3) END FULFILLINGLY. In our treatment of introductions,
we agreed on the necessity of keeping faith with our people.
You invited your hearers to an interesting subject introduced
in an interesting way. This finds fulfillment in the conclusion,
meaningfully and satisfactorily spelled out. Because you
prayed fervently and studied thoroughly, you have not played
around the edges of your theme, but have gone to the very
core of it.

To end at the point of authentic fulfillment enables you
to "quit all over." Not to close fully will leave you unsure
and at loose ends. You have not fulfilled men's expectations,
and to that extent have failed to fulfill your role as God's
messenger.

(4) END EMOTIONALLY. The point requires emphasis, because we live in a day of reaction against the preachers of the past who delighted in committing assault and battery on the emotions. But today we suffer from pulpit tameness. We must once more learn to speak feelingly. Says Paul Sangster, son of the late W. E. Sangster, "Reason is not enough. We do not convince by reason, however cogent; it is only when reason is joined by emotion, when imagination takes the lead, that we convince" (*Speech for the Pulpit*, p. 44). Herein lies one reason modern sermons often are so ineffective.

When people are moved their emotions are called into service. When a person is deeply moved he may, in fact, be motivated to do something about the need which reason has made clear to him. Thus a medical doctor hears preaching about the desperate needs of Burundi, and subsequently finds himself giving three months professional time in an African hospital. A little Irish girl hears the pathetic story of illiteracy in Hong Kong, prepares to teach, and spends three years working with Chinese school children. A dad hears the tragic story of a son, brought up in a Christian home, who, nonetheless, turns his back on the gospel; that father is moved to change his living pattern and spend time creatively with his own son to avoid a similar tragedy.

A word of caution is in order at this point. There are today, as there always have been, men who apparently know little of the causes of psychological trauma, making the human emotions and the subconscious their playfield. The moral implications of playing on that field are clear enough! Of that both history and the modern psychological sciences provide ample documentation. Here it is sufficient to observe the difference between *emotion* and *emotionalism*. The one is emotion in the service of reason; the other is emotion for emotion's sake; the one is good, true, beautiful, and wholesome; the other is sane emotion gone riot.

(5) END PERSUASIVELY. Conclusions must be well grounded. John Wesley convinced powerfully because his training included listening regularly to undergraduate debates at Ox-

ford. He learned well the logic that leads to sound conclusions.

God has frequently chosen men with a background in law to preach the gospel. John Calvin studied law before entering the ministry. Furthermore, some law schools employ the Book of Romans as a model of argumentation.

The minister's task is to reach a verdict, which in homiletics we simply call the "conclusion." It is interesting that the traditional arrangement of the furniture in our churches parallels rather closely the interior of a court room. Thus the very setting of the church lends itself to drawing conclusions or verdicts.

In this connection it is well to remember, however, that some conclusions are reached psychologically more than logically; through feeling more than through pure argument. The difference is illustrated by the argumentation sections of the Epistles as over against the experiential materials of the Psalms, and the Book of Hebrews in contrast to the Book of Lamentations. Learn to appraise sermon content and conclude accordingly, logically or psychologically.

But always remember, conclude to persuade.

(6) END KNOWINGLY. Conclusions frequently depend on facts, theological and otherwise. It is as important to validate data expressed in the conclusion of a sermon, as it is to make sure of the facts given in the body of the sermon.

Suppose you do a homily on some phase of science and religion. Arguing as cogently as you know how, you show that in reality science (*scientia* = knowledge) lives as friend, not foe, of true religion. You are now ready for the clincher and choose for this role a gripping illustration of a world famous scientist, also a devout Christian.

This is good procedure. But in this context, as indeed in any homiletical context, you must be sure of your facts. A scientist, earnestly searching after God, may be present in your audience; an obvious error in that concluding illustration could conceivably turn him away from the gospel to make him say, "Just as I thought. Christians typically lack caution and care in giving facts. I shall have nothing to do with these myth-prone people." The same might be true of college students or others with a knowledge of science.

No preacher has a right to be careless with facts, theological or otherwise, used in his sermons.

Firm up your fact sheet. End knowingly.

(7) END ASSUREDLY. "There are basically two kinds of men in the world," says Peter T. Rohrbach in *The Art of Dynamic Preaching:* "Those who walk timidly on the soles of their feet, and those who walk assuredly on the heels of their feet." One should, of course, walk assuredly on the heels of his feet from beginning to end of the sermon; but if there is one place above another where he *must* walk with assurance, it is the conclusion.

One classic homiletical rule is, Never apologize. Never say something like this: "I could scarcely deliver this message with this awful cold, but to conclude . . . ," or "Sorry I didn't have time to prepare, because. . . ." Let them draw their own conclusions about uncontrollable situations. They will respect you more, and your message will have greater effectiveness.

Some verbalize assuredly but cancel certainty by non-verbal apologies and mannerisms. In the closing moments of the message, never:

> Take out your handkerchief nervously
> Play with your glasses
> Look at your watch (a sure way to lose your audience!)
> Close your Bible
> Open the bulletin for the last hymn

If such nervous behavior is mere habit, do everything in your power to break it. Let all body movement articulate with what is being said; let the whole projection contribute fruitfully to driving home your point.

Conclude on the heels of your feet!

VII. THE PICTURE PRINCIPLE

Albert W. Palmer, first-rate homiletician, said repeatedly, "People do picture thinking." He could not have articulated a more fundamental principle. An Arab proverb, succinct enough, phrases it this way: "He is the best speaker who can turn the ear into an eye." And MacNeille Dixon comes right to grips with the telling difference between the abstract and concrete preachers when he declares, "The mind of man is more like a picture gallery than a debating chamber."

Poets communicate powerfully precisely because they use pictures to bring us in touch with reality. Seldom do they argue without pictures because they are fully aware that naked fact is distant and unrelated to us.

Poets know, too, that pictures constitute the driving forces within us. The subconscious fills and grows with events, actual happenings—all pictures. That is the very nature of remembered experience. Thus an insightful picture identifies with an experience tucked away in the subterranean caverns of the subconscious. The picture becomes deep calling unto deep.

When a speaker gives out abstractions which cannot be seen, there is no point of contact. Exactly here communication falters and finally fails.

PICTURES RELATED TO THE PREACHER'S OWN EXPERIENCE

A. W. Blackwood says one should never preach beyond his own experience. Canned sermon illustrations from omnibus collections seldom ring true in the pulpit. They may sound good on paper, but do they live for the preacher? That is the test. The picture painted must have a point of authentic

107

contact with "my" experience. "I have seen and heard" rings the bell of authenticity.

BIBLICAL PREACHING LENDS ITSELF
TO THE PICTURESQUE

Philosophers, theologians—even many preachers—tend to talk in abstractions. But the Bible abounds in pictures: Moses wrote on tablets of stone; Job suffered nasty, itchy boils; Jonah was captured in the belly of a great fish; Jesus laid His hands on the man's eyes and he could see; Paul was caught in a storm at sea in which some floated ashore on pieces of the battered ship while others swam.

An outstanding literary characteristic of the Bible is its picture quality. Surely this accounts in no small measure for its ability to communicate in any age.

The Bible, born in the Orient where thought and language styles are pictorial, reveals itself as pictographic in character. The preacher's words must be the same.

SOME COMMONALITIES OF PICTURE LANGUAGE

(1) First there is SPECIFICITY. Accuracy of word choice makes for accuracy in the creation of mental images. The preacher's aim is sharpness, vividness. Why describe the snake merely as "long" when you know it was "twenty feet" in length? Why make him "shiny" when he takes on far more reality when you refer to him as "slithery" and "slimy"? Specificity comes, in no small measure, by the use of the adjective.

(2) Be SELECTIVE in your choice of adjectives. Never use adjectives merely for the sake of using adjectives. "Very," "many," "really," tend to dull otherwise sharp images. Portray a person as "very" ill only when he is very ill; refer to "many" books only when that is better than saying "one hundred" books.

(3) Keep ECONOMY ever in mind. Even some otherwise useful adjectives clutter and fog when employed without

discretion. Says Charlie W. Shedd, "The stars do not need ruffles and the most beautiful dress may be spoiled when the petticoat shows. Users of picturesque speech need to pray constantly for a sharp sense of 'just right' versus 'too much.' " Robert Louis Stevenson gives us a rare clue when he observes that, "The great secret of style is to omit."

(4) ENERGY is a universal of picture language. Communicable images are expressed in immediate and active terms, not distant and passive language. Movement, often quick movement, is the genius of cinematic language. This means the craftsman will give studied attention to the actual arrangement of his words. Anyone can say, "Cheer up; things will get better"; but Robert Browning inspires and strengthens with these exciting words, "One who never turned his back but marched breast forward, never doubted clouds would break. . . ." "He worships money," one says; how different to comment, "He daily spreads his prayer carpet toward the First National Bank" (Ralph V. Gilbert, quoted by Charlie Shedd).

(5) POETIC FEEL provides a dimension of picture language. This does not necessarily mean rhyme and rhythm, though they may help; the specific point is a picture's capacity to uncover reality. This is the function of poetry—to reveal. Its role is not so much to argue as to disclose. A preacher should really be a kind of poet. He should be able to take the bud of a good idea and bring it to flower—that is beauty. This will enable him to touch people where they live and feel and hurt—that is reality. It will enable him to paint the struggle of life and offer solutions—that is revelation. The combination of beauty, reality, and revelation provides that feeling tone we call poetry, and it is a universal of effective sermon making.

(6) BEAUTY is a commonality of communicable pictures. As ornamental shrubbery enhances a house, so illustrations accentuate the sermonic truth. Here is a plain building, its color white, its shape square, its decoration nil. In contrast, here is a beautiful building, its color rich and varied, its

shape symmetrical, its decorations in good taste. The one structure communicates so mildly one scarcely notices it; the other, by its impressive beauty, imprints itself indelibly on the human mind.

THE DANGERS OF PICTURE PREACHING

(1) EXAGGERATION holds first place! Preachers possess a penchant for enlarging truth: "evangelistically speaking, he wept buckets of tears." Someone said Samuel Johnson, whose style was to think in very big terms, could not possibly write on a minnow for he would make it a whale.

Part of the genius of really good picture preaching is reserve. Leave something to the imagination of the hearer.

(2) MISREPRESENTATION. Omitting credit where it ought to be given is a pulpit fault. An even worse fault leaves the impression that "this happened to me" when in fact it took place within the scope of another's experience. Subtly shaping the color and tone of a story to suit immediate, even personal, purposes is dishonest. Anything that takes a story out of its natural setting makes it say something unintended.

It is risky to utilize poetry, literature, or narrative not originally written in the context of the Biblical revelation. Never employ an illustration simply because it *sounds* good. Pictures must meet the Christological test: do they point to Jesus, His life, death, resurrection, exaltation, or living presence through the Holy Spirit?

(3) OVER-CREDITING. The preacher must guard against over-quoting and over-crediting.

Identify sources when necessary. If that is necessary often, you quote too much. Pictures right out of life need no literary identification and many actual quotations by famous men such as Shakespeare and the Biblical writers require no singling out. Just quote them. Identify when a borrowed picture could be misconstrued as your own, or when you require the weight of authority to assist in communication.

(4) SUPERFICIALITY is one of the greater risks. The stories

or pictures you use must come to grips with the inner citadel of the soul. This does not exclude pictures used just for fun, or pictures that relieve. But the real, driving illustrations, the kinds of pictures you use habitually, the ones you use to clarify or drive home a truth—these must possess depth. Well-chosen illustrations plow the depths of men's spirits and touch listeners where they bleed.

(5) SOPHISTICATION can threaten the power of an illustration. Gauge your audience. Be sophisticated enough to touch them where they live; do not insult by what to them is simplistic on the one hand, nor above them on the other.

A good deal of modern picture material—song, verse, short story—projects incomprehensible images. Most of us minister to ordinary people. As such we do well to stay close to what is reality for ordinary people. *Saturday Review* records answers British children gave to the question, "What are the loveliest things you know?" The reply of one boy is typical:

> The cold of ice cream.
> The scrunch of dry leaves.
> The feel of clean clothes.
> Water running into a bath.
> Cool wind on a hot day.
> Hot water bottle in bed.
> Honey in your mouth.
> Smell of a drug store.
> Babies smiling.
> The feeling inside when you sing.
>
>> (Quoted by Paul S. Rees in
>> "Concreteness," *How to Prepare
>> and Deliver Better Sermons*)

This is indicative of the need to use illustrations which are real to those whom we wish to reach.

If an illustration requires explaining, do not use it. This is but a reminder of an old homiletical law: *illustrations that need explaining require omitting.*

ASK YOURSELF THESE KEY QUESTIONS

Here, randomly listed, are factors in interrogative form you will want to consider with some care. They are phrased in the first person for immediacy of application.

(1) DO MY ILLUSTRATIONS CLARIFY? The answer is Yes when each illustration zeroes in on a single truth. If the point does not come through loud and clear—if the arrow is left floating in midair—the answer is No. The answer is Yes if the unknown is interpreted by the known; if the unknown attempts to interpret the unknown, the picture fails its intended purpose.

The goal of illustration is revelation, and revelation is impossible without clarification.

(2) DO MY ILLUSTRATIONS FALL IN THE RIGHT PLACES? Spacing illustrations is crucial. Even figures of speech and tiny vignettes need to fall naturally into place. Too many illustrations, or pictures strung together as beads on a string, do not form a sermon; at best that is only entertainment. Moreover, a welter of pictures confuses meanings and the real point, if known, is lost.

Illustrations skillfully spaced have the psychological value of listener relief. An argument cannot proceed very long without the necessity of letup. And if even a little of the-mail-must-go-through spirit surfaces, some kind of breather is required if audience weariness is not to set in. Sometimes—don't overdo it—a light and humorous window will let in the needed fresh air. Clovis G. Chappell demonstrated marked capacity for making people laugh, and his gift for timing—he knew just when to tell a story and when to pick up the ball and go on—assisted materially in making him a classic American preacher.

Spacing also relates to the punch-line effect necessary to drive home a point. Often a picture is required in the climactic position of a sermon section. Indeed, as indicated earlier, the climax of the whole sermon in the conclusion is one of the best places for a gripping illustration.

Sometimes repetition is the best means of driving home a truth. Rather than humdrum redundancies, recasting the point at hand in drama form may do the job. St. Augustine, discussing feedback, advises the preacher to remain ever alert to audience reaction, and to stop when the audience look and slight movement reveal that the point has been made. However, continues Augustine, when the speaker realizes his point has not been made, he must keep at it until success is his. An illustration, even unpremeditated and on-the-spot, may prove to be the most effective way of attaining that goal. Sometimes the preacher will have in reserve an extra story or two for just this purpose.

(3) DO MY ILLUSTRATIONS ASSIST IN THE PERSUASION ENTERPRISE? It is the role of illustrations to convince people of the truth. Word pictures can prove, refute, dissuade, or persuade. Make certain your illustrations really do actually march toward real persuasion of authentic truth. Analogy can be tricky since it has the power to cut both ways; if not cautious, the preacher may find himself in the awkward position of having given the enemies of the gospel an unexpectedly good argument. Tone and tenor of presentation, as well as selection of picture, contribute to the stability of a picture analogy.

(4) DO MY ILLUSTRATIONS REFLECT THE POWER OF SIMILE AND METAPHOR? Jesus was fond of simile: "The Kingdom of God is like a grain of mustard seed." He also put metaphor to good use: "You are the salt of the earth."

Simile says that one thing is *like* another; metaphor says that one thing *is* another. The power of simile and metaphor is the illumination that emerges from demonstrating that *this* is like *that*. Comparison has an almost magic power to light up.

(5) DO MY ILLUSTRATIONS, UNDER ANALYSIS, REVEAL A HEALTHY USE OF BIOGRAPHY? People identify with people; people interpret people. Renowned figures carry weight and authority difficult to find in another source. Moreover, the

full range of Biblical truth is discoverable in the stories of men and women of the past and present.

One caution is in order. Biographical illustration has the potential of robbing the gospel of its full power. If a preacher over-employs life story material, he unwittingly leaves the impression that the Good News is really a man-centered affair rather than a God-centered revelation. Always the Sovereign God, his initiative and penetrating thrust, must loom supreme in the preacher's proclamation. A healthy utilization of biographical material means a modest but steady use of it.

(6) Do MY ILLUSTRATIONS INCLUDE HISTORICAL REFERENCES? Allusions to history suggest that the preacher thinks in depth; preaching stripped of references to the past hints at superficiality. Even in this day and age of revising our attitudes toward the historical, history assists in no small way in interpreting life. Santayana's dictim, "He who refuses to heed the past may be condemned to repeat it," remains a truism for the masses.

Moreover, tradition carries weight. References to Edwards, Finney, and Billy Graham support; those to Jones, Smith, and Mrs. Brown cannot. Westminster Abbey, St. Paul's, and St. Peter's have capacity to underscore truth as the white church on the corner does not.

(7) Then there is the fundamental question all preachers must ask with their critical faculties: Do MY ILLUSTRATIONS EMPLOY EXAMPLE? Few pictures contain greater potential for communication than actual cases in point. It is one thing to exhort your people to be missionaries; it is quite another to relate how Adoniram Judson bore in his own body the marks of cruelty and imprisonment for taking the gospel to Burma. It is even well and good to say there are fifteen hundred boys in the city without a father, but add to that gripping fact the true account of the businessman who started the Big Brother program in the local YMCA. An example wields great power.

But the use of example is subtly dangerous. Exemplifying turns easily to "lecturing" your people, to preaching "at"

them—or to what is readily interpreted as such. They hear
you saying, "Look what so and so has done; why aren't
you doing it, too?" Or, "Observe what a mess he made of
his life; you're going in the same direction." Inevitably this
turns people off. The dynamic principles of homiletics dictate that we prophesy what God commands.

(8) Do MY ILLUSTRATIONS EVER REVEAL IDENTITIES?
Harry Emerson Fosdick made life-situation preaching famous.
His technique was simple. From the counseling room he iden-
tified real-life situations and preached about them, but never
did he identify persons! Problems he revealed, but persons,
never.

"I shall never bare my soul to that preacher," said one,
"for the whole congregation will hear about it in the next
sermon!"

(9) Do MY ILLUSTRATIONS REFLECT THE SUBTLE POWER
OF THE PARABOLIC? Jesus "never spake without a parable."
Why? Hypothetical, and obviously uncalculated to "hit" individuals, the parable is nonetheless suited with laser beam
exactness to striking sin. Its genius is innocency. Innocency
disarms and leaves the hearer open to the penetration of
truth. The Spirit may convict a man quickly and easily with
the parabolic sword.

A parable has a further genius: it is its own explanation.
Point and illustration are one. The preacher, like Jesus, can
start right out with a parable and by its ending everyone has
a grip on the message; or rather, the message has a grip
on the hearers.

What is parable? The classic definition, "an earthly story
with a heavenly meaning," is still satisfactory. A parable is
an enlarged simile or metaphor, as in the simple and beautiful stories of our Lord.

(10) Do MY ILLUSTRATIONS, UNDER CLOSE SCRUTINY,
DEMONSTRATE A SENSIBLE USE OF ALLEGORY? Allegory has
both served and harmed the gospel. A famous example of
service is John Bunyan's *Pilgrim's Progress*, a picture devotional guide second in power only to the Bible. Bunyan had

a gift for personification. Christian, Worldly Wiseman, and all the rest of the characters are "real." So much so that many a preacher, including the well-known John Newton, has capitalized on Bunyan's work, a treasure house of illustration. (Newton did more than one series of lectures on *The Pilgrim's Progress*.) The genius of allegory, sustained personification or representation in narrative, incident, or reference, supplies the triple blessing of understandability, identification, and subtlety. Children make up their own little allegories: the car is Mr. Sputter and, as a real person, he has feelings, reacts, and talks; the two large shrubs on either side of the front door are Jack and Jill, and through the years maintain their identity as "persons." All this has the charm of childhood, from which, happily, adults never quite recover. Preachers do well to take advantage of this to add to the effectiveness of their preaching.

Allegory can, however, be a misleading vehicle of communication. Through the centuries, allegorical exegesis, pioneered by Origen in the ancient church, has attached "spiritual" meanings to Biblical texts quite unintended by the authors or the Spirit of God. For example, the three holy children of Daniel are said to represent the Holy Trinity. Such unwarranted emblematic preaching can leave false impressions of Scriptural truth in the minds of people. Pictures must project honest and natural Scriptural meanings.

(11) DO MY ILLUSTRATIONS DEMONSTRATE AWARENESS OF THE CONTEMPORARY WORLD? An obvious example is space science, with its astronauts, satellite systems, moon walks, and plans for planetary exploration. Young children especially appreciate illustrations in this category, and adults, who always retain something of the adventure of young minds, do as well.

Your witness will be strengthened or weakened according to the degree to which you reflect a real awareness of the world today.

(12) DO MY ILLUSTRATIONS, SOMETIMES AT LEAST, HAVE THE FLAVOR OF THE ARTS? Music, painting, sculpture, archi-

tecture, literature, drama—are all rich resources for the making of images. We must never forget that some people by reason of native endowment and training, migrate toward the gospel and are nurtured in it by the esthetic overtones of our faith. No religion on earth holds so comparable a place as handmaiden of the arts as does Christianity. For the artistically inclined, the classic beauty forms associated with Christianity constitute grand and eloquent authority.

(13) DO SOME OF MY ILLUSTRATIONS REFLECT APPRECIATION OF NATURE? There is a magic to out-of-doors illustration. The man's man as well as the little child and the family-oriented person, find affinity with nature. God is close. The eternity of the mountains, the vastness of the ocean, the far stretches of the sky are God's physical ways of communicating truth about His way of acting. The wind in the trees, the sound of a brook, the roar of a waterfall become God's music to the Christian; they can add music to your sermons, too.

And don't overlook human nature. Your knowledge here is second in importance only to your Biblical grasp. The "law" in Psalms and Proverbs has reference to God's hard-as-nails rules of living—psychological, moral, social, and theological. The alert minister knows man's subtle rationalizings and devious attempts to escape God's law; he knows that men who have learned the law and live by it are happy. Pictures that communicate this dimension of truth with insight and power are of incalculable benefit.

Important in this area is the world of sports. For example, a minister might do well to read *Sports Illustrated*. In this context, he will find himself identifying with many of the men and boys of his audience.

(14) DO MY ILLUSTRATIONS HAVE MERE ENTERTAINMENT VALUE, OR HONEST HOMILETICAL PURPOSE? Many a preacher complains, My people remember stories but not sermons! This is an ever present threat. Stories are both told and listened to easily, far more easily than expository material. Narratives can be so good, so funny, so new, so on the wavelength of

the TV show, the movie, and gossip! Our culture has geared us for entertainment. As a result it is easy for the preacher to allow himself to be shaped into the mold of the world. It is not uncommon for a preacher to address a high school graduating class, only to tell a string of funny stories with absolutely no point!

In this connection one homiletical law remains essential to worthy preaching: *pictures are servants to substance.* Entertainment value must be secondary, never primary.

(15) DO MY ILLUSTRATIONS COME IN A VARIETY OF DRESS? The quickest way to reveal your hobby is in your use of illustrations. Do they tend to come dressed in a baseball uniform? The white jacket of the scientist? The academician's gown? Strive for variety.

Variety, too, must characterize length. Some modern homileticians shun long stories on the premise that in this new, fast and compressed age, people are not geared for them. There may be room and good reason for an occasional five-minute illustration—but not much room! Illustrations need the variance afforded in the wide spectrum of six words to six minutes. In the matter of length, too, *variance* is the point.

Pictures are the windows of your sermon, letting in light. The word *illustration* comes from Latin *illustrare,* "to light up." There is nothing that will do it more efficiently than vivid and varied pictures.

PART THREE:
THE PREACHING

VIII. THE BASES OF PULPIT COMMUNICATION

What are the elements that make preaching truly communicative?

THE GENIUS OF COMMUNICATION

(1) CONCERN. The genius of communication is concern. The greater the degree of concern, the greater the degree of communication.

Ask E. Stanley Jones what his secret of pulpit power is. "I have a deep concern to share Christ," he answers without equivocation. You can feel the throbbing passion to help people in John Wesley's words uttered as he rode into a British town, and recorded in his *Journal*, "I came to bring them Christ." The revolutionary evangelists in the ghettos agree that "love is the key" to communication. Referring to the "I hate Jesus" militants and the Black Muslims, one New York City evangelist said eloquently, "It's not until love is felt that the message is heard" (*Christianity Today*, Oct. 23, 1969, p. 11).

Already we know quite a bit about the budding science of communications. We know, for example, that semantics are important, that word choice can be the difference between turning people off or on, depending on the character and emotion-laden status of terms put into service. We know something about the psychology of communication: mask-wearing deafens; unmasked openness turns up hearing aids. We know something about the atmosphere that gets through to people; its chief characteristic is open acceptance, for when people feel wanted they persuade more easily.

But the crucial point in all this—and here the gospel prin-

ciple of selflessness demonstrates beautifully—is genuine concern. If careful semantics and all the rest of it are "put on,"
quite artificial, even subtly so, your audience will interpret
your motivation not as concern but as conceit. A certain
amount of this may seem harmless in the business community, but in the pulpit the voice of God is blocked off.

In fact, the motivation for learning the more technical
communication skills—voice production, enunciation, and
articulation—is, for the authentic Christian minister, his concern for people. He communicates to help his hearers. If he
communicates to get something out of the experience for
himself, he forfeits even the fringe benefits which are otherwise his.

(2) THE HOLY SPIRIT, SOURCE OF CONCERN. It is one
thing to isolate concern as the genius of communication; it
is quite another actually to demonstrate Christian love. Concern is a gift, a gift that comes into one's life with the coming of the Holy Spirit.

Wayne Oates, in a meaningful article, "The Pastor as
Healer," puts it straightforwardly: "Yet the pastor who moves
at his task as healer without empathy for the hurt of his
people has yet to learn of the Holy Spirit" (*Baker's Dictionary of Practical Theology,* p. 305). If our sermons are to be
truly therapeutic ("salvation" means health), they must carry
that empathic character which is the essence of concern—
and this is a gift of the Spirit of God.

The theological dynamics of this are clear enough. The
nature of sin is pride, the most characteristic expression of
which is selfishness. That propensity to self-reference must
be cleansed, redeemed, and re-channeled by a radical act of
the Holy Spirit. Simultaneous with and subsequent to that
act the Holy Spirit fills us with love which expresses itself
in concern.

With the gift of the Spirit comes the opening of the personality as a channel of God's Presence. The Spirit radiates
through preacher and spoken word. Herein is the Spirit's
secret of communication from Biblical times to the present.

(3) THE TECHNICAL SKILLS FOR PULPIT COMMUNICA-
TION fit into the picture at this point. Conceivably one could
be concerned and gifted by the Spirit, but quite undeveloped
in the sheer physical, social, and psychological skills necessary
to communicate. The concern which the Holy Spirit en-
genders in the preacher's heart provides the motivation to
develop his skills for communicating the Good News. So
motivated, the disciplined preacher will give himself to constant improvement. With the advance of information on every
phase of communication, the opportunity for improvement is
endless.

Communication skills are, to be sure, many and varied,
and skill-oriented statements appear throughout this book.
Key skills not discussed elsewhere find treatment here. Among
them are voice production and projection; pitch, tone, and
appropriate bodily action; enunciation and articulation; pace
and gearing to attention spans.

TECHNIQUES OF COMMUNICATION

(1) VOICE PROJECTION, characterized by life, vibrancy,
and audibility, is of primary importance. If a sermon cannot
be heard, the sermonic effort is wasted; if listening is a
pleasure, power to persuade increases. One study shows that
38 percent of our communication is vocal (Albert Mehrabian,
"Communication Is Vocal," *Psychology Today,* Sept. 1968).
It is, therefore, important to use this phase of communication
to the best possible advantage. Part of the genius of a gospel
communicator like Ethel Barrett is her skillful use of a cultivated voice.

The first secret of projection is to speak to the person in
the back row. If he hears, obviously all will understand. One
preacher put a nail on the back wall of the sanctuary, then
disciplined himself to project to that nail!

A speaker does not need to raise his voice to be heard.
Doing so never pleases an audience, and in this day of micro-
phones it can be annoying and even deafening. Volume is,

of course, a factor, but support must come from the mid-section of the anatomy, not from the throat muscles. This is termed speaking diaphragmatically. The diaphragm is the source of power for voice production.

It is enough to say at this point that proper projection and voice control are the product of the natural and intended use of the vocal mechanism. If you do not know how to put your voice to its best use for effective communication you should consult a good teacher of speech. This may effect a turning point in your pulpit ministry. For many the establishment of new habits emerges rather quickly.

(2) PITCH AND TONE must come in for their share of consideration. The fixing of a communicable vocal image must come from within; never can it be "imposed." An attempt to sound "like a preacher," wise and commanding, ends disastrously. During Harry Emerson Fosdick's heyday, little "Fosdicks" in pulpits across our land attempted to imitate him. Today some, especially young men, try copying Billy Graham. God made us individuals; that unique character in each of us must come to flower. The essense of "vocal sin" is in trying to be something you are not. Naturalness "comes through"; artificiality "misses the boat." In this "conversational" era, people refuse to put up with put-on tones.

We may be conversational but not chatty. Someone has well said that preaching is but a step from prayer; the tone of voice should be shaped accordingly.

The voice should not be pitched beyond its natural median level. Some speakers do this to be heard with greater sharpness, since high tones penetrate the ear better than low. But this causes both serious listener and speaker problems. The listeners may hear too well and feel that the citadel of their own privacy has been invaded beyond acceptable bounds. They have, of course, come to hear the Word of God, but they resist being "clobbered" with it. As for the speaker, voice pathologist Morton Cooper has summed it up vividly enough: "The pinched or tight throat is created by the incorrect use of pitch, tone focus, and breath support. Volume supplied by upper chest support, rather than midsection breath support, exacerbates the voice problem and fatigues the voice faster and more severely." Such vocal behavior, persisted in, can result in serious problems. And Dr. Cooper's observation applies not only to the raising of the voice to unnatural levels, but the misplacing of it in any unnatural position on the scale ("Stopping Vocal Suicide among Preachers"). Indeed, the man whose voice emphasizes "one specific pitch level or area and is stressing one type of tone as opposed to a wider free flow of voice, tone, and pitch" (ibid.) is in fact very much in trouble with both himself and his audience.

Nearly all homileticians have written about unnatural "preacher's" tone, stained-glass speech. Richard Baxter admonished, Forbid it! John Wesley cried out against it, and in his typical analytical way, found four kinds of church tones: (1) "the womanish, speaking tone"; (2) the "singing or canting tone"; (3) the "high, swelling theatrical tone"; and (4) "an odd, whimsical, whining tone." The latter, familiar to us all, was perhaps chiefly in John Newton's mind when he pleaded with his brother ministers and those coming up in the church, to be quite natural.

To sum up, here are two rules worthy of emphasis: (1) find your natural (comfortable) pitch level, making that the median tonal position of your voice; and (2) learn to modulate—the word is important—up and down and around that median. Remember that the voice, a delicate instrument, is best cared for by locating it in its natural position; also keep in mind its potential for shaping meanings by its marvelous flexibility.

(3) ENUNCIATION AND PRONUNCIATION are also key factors in communication. The art of making yourself understood depends not only on volume, pitch, and tone, but also on the formation of sounds. Whitefield could make vast numbers of people hear even a whispered word.

The aim of enunciation is understandability. A pedantic niceness is offensive, as is any spirit of superiority.

Sectionalism constitutes both a hindrance and a handicap. The cockney of London would not do in the typical pulpit because the thickness of the brogue would be likely to make for a corresponding thickness of understanding. Colloquialisms in either accent or phraseology must pass the test of "immediacy" of understanding. The conscientious preacher will want to sharpen his enunciation for the purpose of establishing rapport; anything approaching sounds foreign to accepted culture patterns runs the risk of erecting a "sound" barrier.

A natural and cultivated accent, on the other hand, can actually benefit communication. Few sounds are more beautiful than rich southern speech, and classic Oxford English for much of the world holds highest honors.

For our nation, however, the standard speech is the broadcasting voice, known to all through radio and television. Few preachers attain the quality of vocal articulation and speech enunciation of the announcer because few have the benefit of his training, and not all possess the needed native qualities.

All do, however, have capacities for correct pronunciation. If your habits do not currently dictate carefulness in respect to pronunciation, make lists of words to correct. Your list might include the word *saith* (pronounced like the man Seth, or say-eth), and the book of *Revelation* (no "s"). Give faithful attention to this matter of pronunciation, for both misunderstanding and a poor voice or personality image leave their definite negative consequences. Actually, the minister must be a life-long student of the dictionary to fulfill the responsibilities which God's call has placed upon him. Besides, the preacher really acts as a speech and English teacher, giving instruction by his example—one of the fringe benefits the church has always supplied the community.

(4) One of the most fascinating of communication factors is BODY LANGUAGE, technically known as kinesics. We used to talk about "gesturing." This term has become passé since we have become aware of the fact that the entire body, indeed the entire person, is involved in the communicative

process. Albert Mehrabian tells us that in the person-to-person context, only 7 percent of our communication is verbal, 38 percent is vocal, and 55 percent facial (*Psychology Today, op. cit.,* p. 53). This research apparently assumes the context of a seated situation, as in an office. It would be interesting and useful to see comparable data for the pulpit environment, in which case stance, fingers, hands, arms, the totality of torso involvement would be taken into account in a different way. But the statistics we do have make clear enough how potent nonverbal factors are. Julius Fast, in *Body Language,* has also made that clear.

No longer do we discuss gestures because that implies something artificial, or histrionic. The implications for preaching go far deeper than mere show. Body movement is related to immediate and spontaneous communication from the true heart of the preacher. For example, modern speech psychologists know that, "Facial expression, touching, gestures, manipulation (such as scratching), changes in body position, and head movements—all these express a person's positive and negative attitude, both at the moment and in general, and many reflect status relationships as well" (Mehrabian, p. 54). Again, "The more a person leans toward his addressee, the more positively he feels about him" (ibid.). This, of course, is in the conversation or interview context, but implications for the preacher are clear. The man who feels at home with his people comes through with warmth, communication barriers being down, so that when fingers, hands, and arms move they actually serve to get the message across.

The same kind of thinking applies to eye contact. Classic theatrical speech, even old pulpit rhetoric, taught the studied look; today we know that "the more you like a person, the more time you are likely to spend looking into his eyes as you talk to him" (ibid.). Applied to your church people, they know you are concerned when you look at them "eyeball to eyeball," as the saying goes. When you as a preacher crop your people, looking directly into no one's eyes, you convey distance and miss live contact. When you look at one person the whole congregation identifies—a marvelous fact of audience psychology! Leisurely move from one part of the church to the other, front and back, sides and center, leaving the firm but subconscious impression that you are speaking to everyone and are excluding no one.

When telling a story, look with your mind's eye at the people you point to in the illustration. Point outside the physical scope of all present. Do not point in one direction, only to look in another: that results in a kind of schizophrenic impression, dividing attention, and causing hearers to drop out of the listening enterprise.

This matter of "looking" is extremely important. Just here is the reason manuscript preaching is so hazardous. Eyes give the sense of contact—contact with the audience and contact with the message.

Facial expression is closely related to eye contact, for both assist materially in effecting identification. Whitefield, it is said, had the capacity to bring to his face a thousand moods; what he *said* matched the way he *looked*. Word choice and the tonal shaping of those words help, of course; but how much better to wear the suggestion of anger when discussing anger, and to do the same with sadness—and happiness: don't be afraid to smile; after all, the gospel is a joyous affair.

The same kind of liberation that characterizes the good use of eyes characterizes the whole torso, indeed the very stance of the speaker. The body should move naturally and spontaneously with the mood and picture of the moment. This contributes greatly to the effectiveness of communication. In the best speakers bodily movement works in concert within the total frame of communication.

Billy Graham, a big man, enhances his communication by using great arm movements and holding a sizable Bible. He speaks and moves in large auditoriums and stadiums, and bigger physical environment may require a more expansive circle of bodily operation. Some small men increase the extent of focus by enlarging the radius of arm and body movement. Recently, however, the tendency has been to move suggestively more than grandly. Television has taught us the power of bodily movement in a glance or a slight turn of the head. Generally speaking—though it must be understood that this varies with the personality of the speaker—greater dignity comes with less movement. And in most situations small movements can communicate as well as big ones; indeed, hints sometimes speak with great cogency, as master pantomimists like Marcel Marceau and Red Skelton demonstrate. Such artists are, nonetheless, at perfect liberty to employ the body language necessary to "get through." This is equally your privilege as a preacher.

Intimacy can be achieved in part by standing slightly forward on the balls of the feet. This suggests nearness and provides a sure footing for the speaker. It has the twin psychological effect of lending alertness and enthusiasm to the preacher, factors which create contagion and thus audience participation.

Your arms and hands should rest relaxed at your side when you are not actively communicating. This natural position somehow makes them more available when needed; nervous wringing or rubbing of the hands incapacitates them. Let the hands be at your disposal for any and all needed expressions: an index finger for enumeration or singling out, thumb and fingers brought together for togetherness, the moving arm with open hand for the sweep of a great idea. Only let arm, hand, and finger movement match what is verbalized.

Total body projection we call "presence," and is of immense importance. Marshall McLuhan calls our attention to the total effect of the total communication. What comes over the television is different from what comes by radio because we can *see* it all. Indeed, frequently almost all senses are in use, even smell when the view of something like a steaming cup of coffee suggests it. A "cool" communication is a sensual one, one that uses all or most of the senses; a "hot" communication employs fewer senses. The degree of coolness tends to be the degree of communication.

The tremendous implications of this are clear for preaching. The pulpit communicator is there, Bible and all. He is *visual*, he should be *audible*, and if he is a skillful painter of pictures his communication has great potential for the "cool."

(5) Sensitivity to PACE AND SPACE is important today because of changed circumstances. Formerly the church was the social center of the community. In that day the preacher engaged in quite a different context of work. Just to be together as a community was sufficient reason to go to church, and the preacher in that kind of context could speak at a rather leisurely pace with acceptance.

With the coming of the jet age, we confront an entirely new problem. The number of items fighting for attention makes it more difficult to capture attentions. The capacity to focus, and the length of the attention span, seem to be decreasing, at least when motivation does not demand concentration.

Jerome Bruner, former Harvard psychologist, puts it in scientific language: "The fact of the matter is that the human organism lives normally in a world that is capable of producing more stimulation in the organism than the organism is capable of dealing with. . . . My colleague at Harvard, Professor George Miller, reports that human beings are capable of registering only about 7 plus or minus 2 independent items of information at once. This forces the human nervous system," Dr. Bruner concludes, "into a program of selectivity—with what shall we fill those seven slots?" (Quoted in the *Thomas Jefferson Research Center Monthly Bulletin* for April 1972, 1143 North Lake Avenue, Pasadena, California 91104.)

How, indeed, shall we as preachers of the gospel fill these seven slots? Fillers from the fringes—church architecture, furnishings, flowers, pulpit and altar cloths—all must be such as to contribute to, and help focus on, the gospel message. The sermon itself must fill the slots with worthwhile proclamation and it must be proclaimed at a rate manageable to the hearer—not too fast and not too slow. It is not easy to fill service and sermon with material sufficiently meaningful to command first place in the seven slots, and to hold it at that point more or less consistently throughout the hour of worship.

Listening is hard to command not only because of the competing forces at work, but also because the largest part of communication time in day-to-day existence is spent listening. Dr. Paul Rankin of Ohio State University found that 70 percent of our waking hours are spent in the communication endeavor. Of this, the breakdown shows that 9 percent is used in writing, 15 percent in reading, 30 percent in speaking, and 45 percent in listening. While adults have developed sufficient social skills to keep quiet about their sense of boredom or disinterest, a child expresses the feelings of many adults when he says quite openly, "I'm tired of listening."

Pace and how well space is filled are two important considerations in attaining listening success.

Studies of retention from lecturelike meetings reveal a pretty dismal picture. Only a small percent of information is remembered, and that escapes rapidly soon after. But Jesus knew that an indelible impression can be made in only a few words; it is remarkable that the total words in the Lord's Prayer amount to only fifty-six. Lincoln was shocked when he finally realized what an impact his Gettysburg Address had made; undoubtedly one reason was its brevity—only 266 words. Another example is the Declaration of Independence, containing 300 words. It is no wonder communication was hard going for a recent government order setting the price of cabbage—the order had 26,922 words!

In this connection we should not let the famous and great speakers fool us. John Wesley could speak for an hour, but he forbade his preachers speaking so long. The president of the United States can hold forth as long as necessity demands; but who he is and the importance of his message make his speech world altogether different. And even he, as the careful observer will notice, does not fill space with unnecessary items.

They can do it! The rest of us should size up the situation, determine as nearly as possible how much space to use, and what to put in that space.

Reuel Howe found from actual samplings that pastors tend to carry a load of guilt, fearing they give people insufficient material; the people on the other hand carry a load of frustration attempting to manage too much (*Partners in Preaching*).

If space is crammed full to the breaking point, and if the speaker's pace leaves no room to breathe, communication is sure to stall.

Pace and space—give them your best thought.

(6) Careful attention to ARTICULATION is important to effective communication. As used in this context, enunciation refers to pronunciation and articulation to diction. Articulation relates to words and their arrangement. The most important key to articulation is "plainness of speech." This should not be interpreted as drabness (a whole chapter is devoted to picture preaching), but indicates the importance of simplicity of vocabulary, phrase, clause, and sentence. This will lead you to use words with few syllables, and to make the ground of your vocabulary Saxon rather than Latin. Furthermore, this means that you should keep the number of words in your average sentences low.

Rudolph Flesch developed guidelines by which you can measure the effectiveness of your articulation. Some factors he considers are the average number of words in sentences, the number of affixes per 100 words, and the number of personal references per 100 words.

Sentences averaging 11 words are "easily" understood by 86 percent of American adults, and in this category affixes per 100 words number 26, and personal references 14. This is the pulp fiction level, or fourth grade in the public speech situation.

Seventeen words per average sentence is "standard," and such a construction will communicate to 75 percent of adults, sixth or seventh grade comprehension level in the public speech and listening context. This level has 27 affixes in 100 words, and 6 personal references. This is the *Reader's Digest* level in terms of reading comprehension.

The "very difficult" speech contains 29 or more words to the typical sentence; 54 or more affixes to the average 100 words; 2 or less personal references in every 100 words. Only 4½ percent—they are college and university people—can respond intelligently to this communication structure in the audience context. This is high-level reading matter such as one finds in scientific literature. If you wish more details, consult Flesch's book, *The Art of Plain Talk*.

This research has important implications for the preaching of the gospel. It dictates that the preacher, though a trained man excited about the ideas that filled the fascinating dialog sessions in university and seminary, must reduce his message to an understandable form, and that he will have to hold in abeyance ideas for which his people are not ready. The new graduate may have to alter radically the thought style which he developed during the course of intensive academic training.

You are rushed to the hospital and the doctor simply says you have a broken bone and you immediately know what he means. If in private consultation you show interest in a more sophisticated analysis of your fracture, he will gladly share as much as you wish. In the same way the minister may "theologize" with the interested parishioner, but not in the public preaching setting.

You may wish to check on yourself by Flesch's outline in an effort to measure your own success as a communicator.

IX. THE PREPARATION BEFORE DELIVERY

"Work as if it all depends on you," goes the ancient proverb, "and pray as if it all depends on God." Someone has couched this truth in slightly different terms: "Study without prayer is atheism; prayer without study is presumption." In this balance of study and prayer lies the secret of those hours and moments of preparation between the completed manuscript and the time of entering the pulpit.

WORK AS IF IT ALL DEPENDS ON YOU

Henrietta Mears, long time Director of Religious Education at Hollywood First Presbyterian Church, followed a threefold formula for getting ready for anything—a speech, a banquet, a Sunday school class, whatever:

> Rule 1: Prepare.
> Rule 2: Prepare.
> Rule 3: Prepare.

Her preparation was always with a delightfully buoyant spirit and good humor, but with it all she meant business. Without careful preparation, she could never have been the great Christian leader she was.

You have now come through the earlier steps of preparation: the selection of your theme, and the writing of that theme in a sentence of purpose "clear as a cloudless moon." You have phrased your topic with care, worked through text and context, framed heads and subheads, and arranged data. You have, furthermore, given thoughtful attention to the composition of that first sentence, couched the introduction with all care, and given the same kind of specialized attention to the making of the conclusion. This is all part of the constructional operation.

And where do you go from here? This chapter grapples with that crucial question.

(1) CAPTURE A LISTENING EAR. It may be the ear of a sympathetic friend, a teen-ager, or your wife. It must be someone who will level with you when words, phrases, pictures, and ideas do not come through crystal clear, and when that magic called "immediacy" of comprehension is not there.

Yes, read the manuscript word for word. Dr. Sangster did. Saturday morning was the appointed time, with his wife as the regular listener. And a good critic she was! She made him strike out or alter "any word or phrase or idea which was not immediately clear to her" (*Dr. Sangster,* p. 86).

In the writing of one of his books, Charlie Shedd went over passages with teens. He found the kids reacting realistically, and thus assisting him toward the coveted goal of real communication. After all, we live in a predominantly youth culture. If we can drive the point home to the youngsters we can most probably get through to the oldsters.

(2) EXPERIMENT UNTIL YOU FIND A WORKABLE WAY OF MANAGING YOUR MATERIAL FOR DELIVERY. Part of the business of preparation for sermon presentation is getting ready for delivery itself. In your early years of preaching, you will shape an image for delivery. Bear with yourself patiently while that image takes shape. Once established that image will serve as your model during the hours before delivery.

Now the significant question is, What are the delivery techniques? Some important options follow: they vary in their degree of effectiveness.

Memorizing the manuscript. This technique is recommended only for the very rare person with unusual gifts for memorizing. This technique fails for the ordinary preacher because "rote sound" turns down hearing aids. The human psyche dictates aliveness in the presence of spontaneity; deadness in the presence of calculated discourse. The reason is simple. The preacher who delivers his message with smooth formality appears to be putting whitewash on the fence, slapping it on with great ease, leaving the impression that religion is slick and simple with no sweat or struggle. Identification is broken with real, hurting, knowledge-hungry people. The preacher doesn't seem real to these people who live in a world that is real indeed.

Even if the sermon is memorized and delivered with the finesse of an actor who knows his business, the effect is not desirable. Preaching is not *acting*. Preaching is for real. Man's problem is real and there is a trustworthy solution.

This is not to say that you should never memorize. First and last sentences, even introductions and conclusions on occasion, may well be memorized. Major points should be thoroughly in hand; quotations could often be improved in delivery if memorized. Taking your eyes off your audience to read the quotation can break the spell of attention. Maintaining eyeball-to-eyeball contact, even during quotations, can have the double advantage of heightening speaker-audience contact and increasing hearer respect for the speaker. Here is an inoffensive evidence that the preacher has really prepared, and wants sincerely to communicate.

Poetry and hymns might be memorized to good advantage. Unless it is done very well, a verse read generally falls on deaf ears. Verse directed to the audience from memory, with careful attention to phrasing and inflection, avoiding all impression of artificiality, can be extremely effective.

In short, use this technique of memorizing with discrimination.

Going over the manuscript until the flow is fixed. One man takes his full manuscript into the pulpit to preach "from it," but not to read it. Another does the same, reading only the quotations (he is on radio) but doing that with skill. Still another has before him every line, typed in a rather small loose-leaf notebook. The printed page before each of these preachers constitutes a security symbol—the material "is there" in case it is needed. But none permits himself to enter the pulpit without a thorough mastery of his typescript. None has *memorized,* but all *know* their material.

Still others master the substance of the sermon but take only notes to the pulpit. A full manuscript would hinder these preachers, even with major and minor points clearly underlined. Its very presence would rob them of the feeling of freedom and spontaneity.

Just here is the hazard in any kind of careful mastery of manuscripts. Mastered they must be, but if this gives the impression of memorization, the preacher finds himself in the same ineffective position as the rote speaker. Reality, authenticity, genuineness—these are the sensitive preacher's watchwords.

The young preacher may have to exercise patience with himself while learning to master materials and to maintain spontaneity at the same time. He may, in fact, go through a period of overmastery. This he can detect from audience feedback, both verbal and non-verbal. Then he will patiently, carefully, gradually reshape his delivery until feed-back normalizes.

Mastering ideas and pictures. This is the best of all possible methods of preparation for delivery. The perspective is entirely different. This is not a word-and-phrase oriented technique; it is a picture-and-idea orientation. Words are left to fend for themselves, as it were; and if you have been careful in the preparation of your typescript, the words will fend and fare far better than you would have imagined! It is surprising how many actual phrases and word sequences come back to you when you are not trying so hard. The great gift of the public speaker who has done his home work is his memory bank, called the subconscious.

You need not worry if words do not fall just where you planned. They may fall better than you had planned! Communication seems to flower better in the spontaneous context, even when phraseology is not so perfect as one had wished.

The psychological dynamics of this technique are explained in part by the fact that words cluster better around ideas and pictures than they do around words. Great ideas and vivid illustration are like magnets to words; sometimes the words even come rushing and tumbling. This pattern is related to the basic motivation in the speaker. If he has mastered concepts and images rather than words and phrases, it is more likely that he sees his real goal to be helping people rather than producing an art masterpiece. And it may well be that he can actually come nearer his masterpiece in the more flexible speaking context. The fact is that the average listener would much rather experience living communication than hear a pretty essay. He finds the spontaneous speaker contagious, identifies with him, and leaves with the feeling that the message was directed to him personally, and that it has done him good.

With all its genius, one major warning should be issued in connection with the use of this method. It is this: laziness, stealthy as it is, has a way of creeping into a man's work habits. How easy simply to list on a half-sheet a few ideas and illustrations, and stride to the pulpit with full confidence in your gift of talking. Use these jottings a second and a third time, and you find that your message charged with creativity and enthusiasm at one time, is now hackneyed! Thin content, untidy organization, threadbare illustrations— three demons that rear their ugly heads—will quickly take command in the busy preacher's study if his sentries are not vigilant.

Herein, too, is the great danger of preaching without notes. If one can do it with freshness of content and style, and excitement in delivery, all well and good! But rare is the man who can actually bring that off.

A happy medium between preaching without notes and using a full manuscript, is the carefully done note sheet including date, place, occasion of message, topic, text, key reminder words for introduction, points and sub-points, and conclusion. Depending on one's skills and the amount of material, the note sheets may number one or several. Generally the more seasoned speaker requires fewer notes. Whenever possible, employ just one to three words as reminders of the idea or picture about which you will talk.

Half-sheets are better than cards—especially 3 x 5 cards, which are small, contain little, and are easily lost in the shuffle. Readability is supremely important, and your notes should be geared to the quick glance. Many words on a line tend to prohibit fast reading; crowding does the same. Space is the key to quick-as-a-flash readability.

Half-sheets move easily and imperceptibly (curb the temptation to neaten up your sheets!), and should simply be slipped across the lectern. You should keep the half-sheet high on the lectern so that when you do look at your notes, eye contact is less likely to be lost. A piece of felt on the lectern will help hold notes in place. Cards tend to slide to the bottom of the lectern, forcing you either to push them back to the top or to look down when consulting them.

Over the years you will develop your own technique for underscoring, circling, penciling in color—depending on the technique you prefer. Some kind of emphasis code system, known perfectly to yourself, needs developing. This aids quick readability, and impresses on your own mind the kind of impact you want to leave with your hearers.

Reading, almost without exception, is the worst possible technique of delivery. Only the very rare public speaker can read a sermon well and effectively. A corporation president reads his addresses because of their technical character, and he can get away with it better because of the total context in which he works. But the preacher is in a quite different environment. An I-Thou encounter between Word and listener is the preacher's goal. Unless one has the powerful machine-gun delivery of a Phillips Brooks or, like Jonathan Edwards delivering "Sinners in the Hands of an Angry God," is set aflame by the Spirit, reading simply will not effect the desired contact.

There are, of course, exceptions to everything. Occasionally one hears of a preacher who has learned to read feelingly. He may be a man who has no choice: he simply lacks fluency and is thus forced to learn to read publicly. Hopefully he will yet learn to do other than read, for indeed he may be a shy young man only now developing into a speaker. Happy the man who develops, for in committees, at picnics, with informal groups, he will be called on regularly to preside or "say a few words."

If you must read, for part or all of your preaching career, then you should follow guidelines. First, you would do well to find access to a scriptwriter, a typewriter with very large letters. This has the obvious advantage of heightening readability. IBM produces a scriptwriter ball attachment for the Selectric machine. Until you can locate a scriptwriter, triple space typescript and use caps as freely as necessary. Second, use only the top half of 8½ x 11 sheets if that is the size sheet you prefer, so that at no point are you losing eye contact with the congregation. Third, catch the feel (this may take a bit of seasoning) of reading publicly. The newscaster has had to catch this feel, though the voice he has developed projects a news image. Obviously, yours must be somewhat different. If you are going to communicate you must project naturally and feelingly and meaningfully. Fourth, resist the temptation of complex and flowery sentence structure; this only compounds communication problems. Keep sentences short without being staccato (a subtle varying of length is the trick). Bear in mind the imperative of immediacy. Employ color and contrast; put legs and feet to your ideas so they possess power to run without falling and to walk without fainting.

Unless you *must* read—and some may have to for two or three years—don't. Reading is a much more difficult method of delivery since reading skills are harder to come by than natural speech expertise.

(3) THOSE LAST HOURS AND MINUTES BEFORE DELIVERY. Through experimentation you will have to discover the best plan for you. Ralph G. Turnbull, while in the pastorate, completed his sermon by midweek, let it soak, reviewed frequently, and typed his outline from memory Saturday night

("If I can type it, I can preach it without notes"). The ten minutes between church school and 11 o'clock worship were reserved for absolute quiet. That "absolute quiet" is essential, and we shall come back to it.

Stephen Olford reserved all of Saturday for study, meditation, brooding, and prayer in his work room; no one, not even his wife, could get to him. Before he preached to Richard Nixon and Billy Graham, he spent the night in prayer.

The mind has its laws. One is the necessity of calm before the storm, so to speak. An eye surgeon never allowed himself the luxury of excitement the night before an operation. Olford and Turnbull hit onto something fundamental, each after the individual makings of his own mind, when they insist on peace and quiet before preaching. There must be such calm periods throughout the week too. Gossip walked in his garden; F. W. Robertson retired to his study; Edwards rode his horse into the woods.

Not unrelated is the law of the mind that dictates "forgetting it all" at some point (perhaps Saturday) before delivery. Come to rest about the whole thing; forget it; find diversion— a football game, your stamp collection, anything. A Seattle talk show team insists on preparing two weeks ahead of broadcasting so that ideas may have a chance to simmer. When the time for the show itself comes, spontaneity, freshness, and excitement characterize their talk.

If you cannot forget, you are in trouble. Then you will have to learn to turn off your mind, and turn it on to something altogether different than your sermon theme. Besides, this gives your subconscious a chance to sort things out, arrange, and get in tune before actual delivery time comes.

The wise man obeys the laws of the mind.

PRAY AS IF IT ALL DEPENDS ON GOD

"The knowledge of the priest is the eighth sacrament of the church," said Francis de Sales with justification. The awareness of what happens to the priest in prayer is perhaps the most significant phase of that knowledge.

(1) THE FIRST THING THAT HAPPENS TO HIM IS GOD. Waiting quietly in His presence is step number one to God's breaking through. The relation of His presence to power in preaching can almost be put into a formula: The greater the degree of God's presence the greater the degree of spiritual power in the preaching of His Word. We dare not and cannot reduce God to a formula. God moves when, where, and how he wills, says the Westminster Catechism. But having said all that, the fact remains that spiritual sensitivity and receptivity can be learned.

Surrender, complete abandonment of self to God, is the first law of receptivity. Surrender is not learned easily; original sin prevents us growing up with the capacity of total commitment. But learn it the minister must! Without it he fails.

Cleansing is another law of the presence of God. Even as the Old Testament priest could not enter the Holy of Holies without spiritual washing, so today's priest dare not enter the Lord's holy sanctuary and preach the eternal Word without fresh cleansing. Simply ask God for it in all sincerity; He answers with astonishing readiness.

The new anointing of His Spirit is yet another law of prayer. There is, of course, the initial filling of the Spirit discussed earlier in this volume; but there are, of necessity, subsequent fillings. The man of God has many such fillings which we call anointings. In anointing God separates and sanctifies, sets apart and makes ready, His instrument for service. To be sure, this was done initially; now it is done again, freshly for the specific preaching occasion just ahead.

That—rather, God—is the foremost benefit of prayer.

(2) THE FRESH AWARENESS THAT GOD IS IN CHARGE constitutes a highly significant knowledge. There is a deep sense in which this theological fact, truly believed, gets one right off the hook. Only half believe it and you may get uptight about service and sermon. Many is the time a good case of nerves is nothing more nor less than spiritual in origin. Perhaps this relates to Paul's meaning when he admonishes

Christians not to "think of themselves more highly than they ought to think." If the preacher thinks he is pretty good after all, he will begin to shoulder the total burden of responsibility; and when he discovers he cannot do that successfully by himself, much less bring off every sermon with any kind of brilliance, he is beside himself.

Never did Paul say, "I can do all things." He said, "I can do all things through Christ who strengthens me." There is a vast difference, and the awareness of that difference and, more important, the strength that actually comes from Christ are found on one's knees. True *humility* emerges from this crucial knowledge.

The preacher is a trumpet, God's instrument. God will neither keep the trumpet shined nor in tune, but if we fully surrender the instrument to Him He will produce music both telling and touching. No preacher has power to convince, convict, and convert; that function God Almighty reserves for Himself.

This great fact, freshly and firmly rooted and grounded in the soul of God's servant, also gives him that incomparable quality of witness, *serenity.* This is a quality that has power to communicate nonverbally, and projects itself to the audience almost immediately. When people see it they see God; they see living proof that God can bring peace. After all, God is the real sermon preached.

There is another quality that marks the man who has learned that God is in charge—*confidence.* This should not be confidence in oneself so much as confidence in God, the authentic source of a proper self-confidence. Try all the tricks in the book to drum up self-confidence; they sooner or later end in failure. Find God and discover the confidence that results from trust in Him. The sure knowledge that God is God, is the supreme source of the trusting spirit, and like serenity it is almost immediately detectable. The spiritually sensitive do in fact detect it at once; those who are infants in the faith sense it less; but even those still outside the realm of Christian experience have some capacity of recognizing the source and character of the minister's confidence.

Humility, serenity, confidence—these three indispensable qualities make or break sermon and service. The man patiently dedicated to learning how to pray will discover this golden secret sooner than he knows.

(3) PRAYER ATTUNES THE MINISTER TO GOD'S VOICE. In Germany with my family on a summer's holiday, we were driving through the richly greened countryside when a farm loomed into view. The whole scene, lovely and picturesque, made it impossible to resist stopping. The quiet captured us and held us fast. Then we heard it; rather, *they* heard it! A cuckoo sang. I listened at the family's insistent instruction. But so many other birds sang, and the wind in the tall trees made its own music: all competed against the cuckoo. Then at one last word of guidance, I heard it. That was a choice moment indeed. There it was, the song that made the clocks of the Black Forest known the world over.

Yes, it does take a bit of instruction, and most particularly quiet patience, to learn to detect the Voice of God. But what rewards when learned! His Voice articulates with the truth in Holy Scripture—that first and foundationally—and it harmonizes with what the Church has said down through the ages in its creeds and hymns. And somehow, after all that, it articulates with the inner voice. The test of the validity of that inner voice, in addition to tests listed above, is the cessation of inner disquiet. When the debating ends—indeed, sometimes it never begins—we may be sure that the Voice is God's.

Thus, on one's knees the preacher may be led to change a point or sequence. He may in fact be led while in the pulpit, quite spontaneously and on the spot, to alter a declaration or an illustration. Flexibility to do so is the fruit of prayer.

God speaks in another way. In a somewhat indirect way. He speaks to His servant through His people. Often the minister knows of individual hurts in his congregation, and these he will tactfully and prayerfully attempt to heal through the preached word. But he will also be sensitive to the mood of the gathered church at any given service of worship. To sense the atmosphere and become the channel of God's Word in that setting will result in productive contact at deep levels. During the course of the sermon, and very often during the last words and closing prayer after the sermon, the minister will be especially sensitive to God's inner voice.

(4) PRAYER FIRES THE PREACHER, and puts within him that indispensable urgency without which no sermon communicates. And it is noticeable. There is a divine imperative about him as he enters the pulpit; he *must* declare God's Good News. He enthuses (*enthusiasm* comes from *en theos,* "in God") as Jeremiah the prophet who had fire in his mouth, and as Isaiah whose lips were touched with a burning coal from off the altar. Jesus said He came to bring fire on the earth. The history of preaching is replete with men ignited by His flame. Martin Luther would even preach from an upstairs window; Wesley declared the mighty acts of God from doorway or tombstone; Whitefield's sense of urgency was so great he preached to the people gathered at the bottom of a stairway, weak though he was, before he went to his bed for the last time.

The contemporary preacher, living in the modern and erudite space age, knows ignition is requisite to getting airborne. Thus Harold John Ockenga came to a meeting of the National Association of Evangelicals to open his address feelingly with the words, "Tonight I have a hot heart." Billy Graham wrote a book called *World Aflame,* and the very title symbolizes the dynamic which characterizes that man's prophetic preaching. Indeed, any contemporary, no matter who he is, communicates the Word only when fired.

It is difficult to imagine how any man genuinely called of God to preach the transforming Word of God, can mount the pulpit as if nothing were about to happen. The fact is just this: the service at hand may prove the turning point in someone's life. This may be the hour for a distressed wife and mother to discover a way out of her domestic troubles; this may be the service to turn a tempted but malleable teen to Christ for both earthly and eternal life; this may be the time a senior citizen experiences release from loneliness. Then in God's name, let us pray until we are baptized in the fire that propels us into the pulpit with lips aflame and tongues of fire.

GENERAL HINTS FOR PREPARATION

(1) KEEP YOUR MIND SHARP AND ALERT. One man reads well-written literature while in a mood to write; models stimulate the best from his pen. By the same token, a preacher does well to expose himself to excellent models of communication before preaching. Thus one man reads or talks with a good mind on Saturday night before preaching Sunday morning. "Iron sharpens iron, and one man sharpens another" (Prov. 27:17).

(2) KEEP YOUR BODY FIT. The best minds are housed in the best bodies. Billy Graham runs and Paul Rees golfs (as a young man he played tennis). The fit body relaxed is the body released of tensions and fatigue, and is thereby prepared for clear and quick brain work. Sluggish bodies and sluggish thinking are Siamese twins.

(3) REST YOUR BODY. Fatigue toxins are also diminished in sleep; conversely they accumulate in long hours of work and confinement. One minister excuses himself when the party gets too late; it is time for evening prayers and sleep! Another errs miserably with too much fun, or lengthy theological dialog—perhaps in the name of social nicety. After all, it is possible for the minister to excuse himself with grace! The issue is gumption as well as grace—especially the night before preaching.

(4) TAILOR YOUR DIET. One minister learned that only a light breakfast permitted clear thinking and fluent speech at 11 o'clock; another discovered he was made to consume a hearty breakfast to supply energy demands. Study diet; experiment until you know what works to bring your energy sources to optimum level. The preacher-in-action uses energy supplies at rates higher than he may know.

(5) WORSHIP WHOLEHEARTEDLY WITH YOUR PEOPLE.
If you reserve yourself for the sermon you will miss identification with your people. The people know whether or not
you are worshiping with them. Sing enthusiastically as unto
the Lord—this releases nervous tension, too!—and read the
Scriptures feelingly. Let the people be fully aware of your
gladness to be with them, and that so far as you are concerned there is nothing on earth so meaningful and reward-
ing as the corporate worship of God. If the leader is a wor-
shiper he is the better leader; and he will be by far the better
preacher—because preaching is a form of worship. Preaching is one's sacrifice on the altar, consumed by a fire from
heaven; and the smoke from that altar is a sweet smelling
savor to Almighty God.

BIBLIOGRAPHY

Allmen, Jean Jacques von (ed.). Introduction by H. H. Rowley; translated from the second French edition by P. J. Allcock and others. *A Companion to the Bible.* New York: Oxford University Press, 1958.

Allport, Gordon W. *Personality, A Psychological Interpretation.* New York: Henry Holt and Company, 1937.

Atlas of the Bible Lands. Maplewood, New Jersey: C. S. Hammond & Company, Inc., 1959.

Barclay, William. *A New Testament Wordbook.* London: SCM Press, 1955.

————. *More New Testament Words.* New York: Harper & Brothers, 1958.

————. *The Daily Study Bible Series* (commentaries on the New Testament books). Philadelphia: Westminster Press, 1953 and following.

————. *The Master's Men.* London: SCM Press, 1959.

Bauman, J. Daniel. *An Introduction to Contemporary Preaching.* Grand Rapids: Baker Book House, 1972.

Baxter, Batsell Barrett. *The Heart of the Yale Lectures.* Grand Rapids: Baker Book House, reprinted 1971 (Copyright 1947 by the Macmillan Company), with an Introduction by Ralph G. Turnbull.

Black, James. *The Mystery of Preaching.* London: James Clarke & Company, Limited, 1934.

Black, Matthew (ed.) and H. R. Rowley (O.T. ed.). *Peake's Commentary on the Bible.* London: Thomas Nelson and Sons, Ltd., 1962.

Bonhoeffer, Dietrich. *The Cost of Discipleship.* Trans. by R. H. Fuller with some revision by Irmgard Booth. New York: Macmillan, 1959.

Brooks, Phillips. *On Preaching.* (The Yale Lectures on Preaching for 1877.) London: SPCK, 1965.

Bruce, F. F. *Commentary on the Book of Acts; the English Text With Introduction, Exposition and Notes.* (The New International Commentary on the New Testament.) Grand Rapids: Wm. B. Eerdmans Publishing Company, 1954.

Buttrick, George A. (ed.). *Interpreter's Dictionary of the Bible.* Nashville: Abingdon Press, 1962. 4 volumes.

Christianity Today. Harold Lindsell, Editor-Publisher. Published fortnightly by Christianity Today, Inc., 1014 Washington Building, Washington, D.C., 20005.

Decision. Sherwood E. Wirt, Editor. Published monthly by The Billy Graham Evangelistic Association, 1300 Harmon Place, Minneapolis, Minnesota, 55440.

Dodd, C. H. *The Apostolic Preaching*. New York: Harper, 1950.

Douglas, J. D. (ed.). *The New Bible Dictionary*. London: The Inter-Varsity Fellowship, 1962. (Published in America by Eerdmans.)

Farmer, H. H. *The Servant of the Word*. Philadelphia: Fortress Press, reprint from 1942 Scribner's edition (The Preacher's Paperback Library, Edmund A. Steimle, Consulting Editor).

Flesch, Rudolf. *The Art of Plain Talk*. New York: Collier Books Edition, 1971.

————. *The Art of Readable Writing*. New York: Collier Books Edition, 1962.

Fox, George. *Journal*. London: Thomas Northcott, 1694. (N.Y.: AMS Press, 1972).

Harper, A. F., and others (eds.). *Beacon Bible Commentary*. Kansas City: Beacon Hill Press, 1969. 10 volumes.

Hastings, Edward (ed.) and James Hastings (founder). *The Speaker's Bible*. Grand Rapids: Baker Book House, 1963 reprint. 36 volumes.

Hastings, James (ed.). Revised edition by Frederick C. Grant and H. H. Rowley. *Dictionary of the Bible*. New York: Scribner, 1963.

How to Prepare and Deliver Better Sermons. Washington, D.C.: Christianity Today, n.d.

Howe, Reuel L., *Partners in Preaching*. New York: Seabury Press, 1967.

Jones, E. Stanley. *Christ at the Round Table*. London: Hodder and Stoughton, 1928.

————. *Victory Through Surrender*. Nashville: Abingdon, 1966.

Jowett, J. H. *The Preacher: His Life and Work* (Yale lectures). Grand Rapids: Baker Book House, 1968 reprint of 1912 edition, introduction by Ralph G. Turnbull.

Kittel, Gerhard. *Theologisches Wörterbuch Zum Neuen Testament*. Translation under title *Bible Key Words* by various authors. London: Adam and Charles Black, several volumes (Apostleship, Church, Faith, etc.) published at various times.

Kittel, Gerhard and Geoffrey W. Bromiley (trans. and ed.). *Theological Dictionary of the New Testament*. Grand Rapids: Wm. B. Eerdmans Publishing Company, 1964 following (multi-volume work still in process).

Kraeling, Emil G. *Rand McNally Historical Atlas of the Holy Land*. New York: Rand McNally & Company, 1959 (paperback edition).

Lewis, Ralph L. *Speech for Persuasive Preaching*. Wilmore, Kentucky: Speech Department, Asbury Theological Seminary, 1968.

Lloyd-Jones, D. Martyn. *Preaching and Preachers*. Grand Rapids: Zondervan Publishing House, 1971.

Matthews, Eunice Jones, and James K. Matthews. *Selections from E. Stanley Jones, Christ and Human Need*. Nashville: Abingdon Press, 1971.

Morgan, George Campbell. *The Ministry of the Word*. Grand Rapids: Baker Book House, 1970 (reprint of the 1919 edition with a new introduction by Ralph G. Turnbull).

Mounce, Robert H. *The Essential Nature of New Testament Preaching*. Grand Rapids: Eerdmans, 1960.

Nespur, Paul W. *Biblical Texts*. Minneapolis: Augsburg Publishing House, 1952.

Nichols, Sue, and art by Doyle Robinson. *Words on Target*. Richmond: John Knox Press, 1963.

Nicole, W. Robertson (ed.). *The Expositor's Greek Testament*. London: Hodder & Stoughton, 1897-1910. Reprint: Grand Rapids: Wm. B. Eerdmans Publishing Co., 1970. 5 volumes.

Pfeiffer, Charles F. *Baker's Bible Atlas*. Grand Rapids: Baker Book House, 1961.

Richardson, Alan (ed.). *A Theological Word Book of the Bible*. London: SCM Press, Ltd., 1950.

Robertson, Archibald Thomas. *Word Pictures in the New Testament*. New York: Harper, 1932. 6 volumes.

Sangster, Paul E. *Doctor Sangster*. London: The Epworth Press, 1962.

———. *Speech in the Pulpit*. London: The Epworth Press, 1958.

Sangster, W. E. *Power in Preaching*. London: The Epworth Press, 1958.

———. *The Craft of the Sermon* (combines two earlier publications, *The Craft of Sermon Construction* and *The Craft of Sermon Illustration*). London: The Epworth Press, 1968 printing. Separate volumes reprinted (paperbacks in Notable Books on Preaching) by Baker Book House.

Selwyn, Edward Gordon. *The First Epistle of St. Peter. The Greek Text with Introductions, Notes and Essays*. London: Macmillan & Co., Ltd., 1946.

Stewart, James S. *A Faith to Proclaim*. New York: Charles Scribner's Sons, 1953. Paperback reprint by Baker Book House, 1972.

———. *Exposition and Encounter: Preaching in the Context of Worship*. Birmingham, England: The Berean Press, 1956.

———. *Heralds of God*. London: Hodder and Stoughton, 1946. Paperback reprint by Baker Book House, 1972.

———. *River of Life*. Nashville: Abingdon Press, 1972.

———. *The Gates of the New Life*. Edinburgh: T. & T. Clark, 1937. Paperback reprint by Baker Book House, 1972.

———. *The Life and Teaching of Jesus Christ*. London: SCM Press, 1958. (In U.S.A. Abingdon.)

———. "The Lord God Omnipotent Reigneth," in *The Protestant Pulpit* edited by Andrew W. Blackwood (Nashville: Abingdon Press, 1957). Available in paperback.

————. *The Strong Name.* Edinburgh: T. & T. Clark, 1940. Paperback reprint by Baker Book House, 1972.

————. *Thine Is the Kingdom.* Edinburgh: The Saint Andrew Press, 1956.

Stott, John R. W. *The Preacher's Portrait, Some New Testament Word Studies.* London: Tyndale Press, 1961. (Eerdmans in America.)

Temple, William. *Readings in St. John's Gospel.* (First and Second Series). London: Macmillan and Company, Limited, 1950.

The Book of Common Prayer and Administration of the Sacraments and Other Rites and Ceremonies of the Church, According to the Use of the Protestant Episcopal Church in the United States of America, Together with the Psalter of Psalms of David. New York: Harper & Brothers, 1944.

Thomas, Jefferson Research Center Monthly Bulletin for April 1972. (Address: 1143 No. Lake Ave., Pasadena, California 91104).

Toohey, William and William D. Thompson. *Recent Homiletical Thought: A Bibliography, 1935-1965.* Nashville: Abingdon Press, 1967.

Turnbull, Ralph G. *Baker's Dictionary of Practical Theology.* Grand Rapids: Baker Book House, 1967.

Walls, Andrew F. *A Guide to Christian Reading, A Classified List of Selected Books.* London: Inter-Varsity Fellowship, 1965 (3rd ed.).

Wright, George Ernest and Floyd Vivian Filson (eds.). *The Westminster Historical Atlas to the Bible.* Philadelphia: The Westminster Press, 1946 (revised 1956).

Young, Robert. *Analytical Concordance to the Bible . . . Containing About 311,000 References, Subdivided Under the Hebrew and Greek Originals, With the Literal Meaning and Pronounciation of Each.* Revised by Wm. B. Stevenson, and a new supplement, "Recent Discoveries in Bible Lands" by William F. Albright. Grand Rapids: Wm. B. Eerdmans Publishing Company, 1952.

INDEX